FREEDOM
IN CHRIST

Participant's Guide

THE
GRACE
COURSE

An **8-Session Guide** to Experiencing
Freedom and Fruitfulness in Christ

STEVE GOSS

& Freedom In Christ Ministries

BETHANYHOUSE
a division of Baker Publishing Group
BethanyHouse.com

ISBN 9780764242342

Unless otherwise indicated, Scripture quotations are from The Holy Bible, English Standard Version® (ESV®), copyright © 2001 by Crossway, a publishing ministry of Good News Publishers. Used by permission. All rights reserved. ESV Text Edition: 2016

Scripture quotations marked CSB are taken from the Christian Standard Bible®, copyright © 2017 by Holman Bible Publishers. Used by permission. Christian Standard Bible® and CSB® are federally registered trademarks of Holman Bible Publishers.

Scripture quotations marked ERV are taken from the HOLY BIBLE: EASY-TO-READ VERSION © 2014 by Bible League International. Used by permission. https://www.bibleleague.org/bible-downloads/license-agreement/

Scripture quotations marked LSB are taken from the Legacy Standard Bible Copyright ©2021 by The Lockman Foundation. All rights reserved. Managed in partnership with Three Sixteen Publishing Inc. LSBible.org

Scripture quotations marked NASB are taken from the (NASB®) New American Standard Bible®, Copyright © 1960, 1971, 1977, 1995, 2020 by The Lockman Foundation. Used by permission. All rights reserved. www.lockman.org

Scripture quotations marked NASB 1995 are taken from the (NASB®) New American Standard Bible®, Copyright © 1960, 1971, 1977, 1995 by The Lockman Foundation. Used by permission. All rights reserved. www.lockman.org

Scripture quotations marked NIV are taken from the Holy Bible, New International Version®, NIV®. Copyright © 1973, 1978, 1984, 2011 by Biblica, Inc.® Used by permission of Zondervan. All rights reserved worldwide. www.zondervan.com. The "NIV" and "New International Version" are trademarks registered in the United States Patent and Trademark Office by Biblica, Inc.®

Cover Design: Studio Gearbox

Author Photo: © Rebecca Moye

24 25 26 27 28 29 30   7 6 5 4 3 2 1

COMMENTS FROM PARTICIPANTS

"The awesomeness of God runs through this course—
we can all come to the knowledge that
we have been set free by grace."

"For the first time in the decades I've been a Christian,
I'm suddenly 'getting' it—that actually
this is *grace* and it is amazing."

"*The Grace Course* has introduced Christ back into my life,
knowing that I love Him and He loves me."

"Understanding that it's not about my performance but He
just wants my heart is what blew me away. It's great!"

"*The Grace Course* helped me to realize that there is nothing
I can do to make God love me more or love me less,
and to choose to serve Him purely out of love."

"It brings out truths that have been hidden
to so much of the Church for so long."

"During the course I felt a progressive lifting,
the burden just going, and I feel so light now."

"All of the presenters shared what happened to them
and that honesty really comes across."

"It was so refreshing to enjoy, delight and soak in
the truth of God's Word and receive it in my heart."

Contents

INTRODUCTION
WHY TAKE PART IN THIS COURSE?

Do you want to keep growing as a Christian, and bear more and more fruit that will last forever? By God's grace—and only by His grace—you can! The objective of *The Grace Course* is to help you experience God's grace in such a deep way (in your heart as well as your head) that love for Him becomes the main motivator in your life.

Here's a flavor of what you will learn:

- how to deal with the false motivators of guilt, shame, fear, performance, and pride;
- why doing things for God because you feel you have to is worth precisely nothing;
- how to get rid of that "low grade fever" of guilt in your life;
- that you can hold your head up high no matter what's in the past;
- you need fear nothing and no one except God Himself;
- how to deal with sins that grip you;
- how to operate in the authority of Jesus to disciple the nations;
- the true meaning of unity and why it is so important;
- that if you want to be really fruitful, it starts with resting and brokenness;
- how practically to renew your mind so that you will be transformed.

As you experience His grace like never before, our expectation is that you will go on to bear more fruit than you ever thought possible!

HOW CAN I GET THE MOST OUT OF IT?

Do your best to get to each session and catch up with any you have to miss (ask your group leader for access to the video if available).

Use the YouVersion devotional on The Bible App, which will accompany you through this course (see page 8).

Ensure you take the opportunity to go through *The Steps To Experiencing God's Grace*, a kind and gentle process during which you ask the Holy Spirit to show you any areas of your life where you may need to repent.

The course includes strategies for standing firm in the freedom won and renewing your mind on an ongoing basis—make them part of your daily life.

As you become aware of areas where your thinking is not in line with biblical truth, write them in the Lies List at the end of the book and work out what is actually true from God's Word.

You will be introduced to "Stronghold-Busting," a straightforward and very effective strategy for renewing your mind (see Romans 12:2) that will help you deal with the lies you uncover and stand firm in your freedom. Make it part of your daily life.

Read the accompanying books to reinforce the teaching.

MAKE YOUR *GRACE COURSE* EXPERIENCE EVEN BETTER!

The Grace Course is at the heart of *The Grace And Freedom Project*, a collaboration between a number of leading producers of discipleship and devotional resources.

That means there are some wonderful additional resources you can take advantage of as you go through *The Grace Course*. Read about them below. Scan the QR code to find out more or go to:

www.GraceAndFreedomProject.com

THE WONDER OF GRACE VIDEO SERIES

An 8-session series of short, punchy videos presented by Sidhara Udalagama that cover key themes from *The Grace Course*. The themes of the sessions correspond to the *Grace Course* sessions. We recommend you watch them in the days before each session—they will give you a great introduction to what we will be looking at and get you thinking!

Available to stream from Freedom In Christ's Discipleship Hub (no additional charge for those who have access to *The Grace Course* videos on the platform), and from RightNowMedia.

DAILY NUGGETS OF GRACE YOUVERSION DEVOTIONAL

A 56-day (8-week) daily devotional designed to accompany you on your journey through *The Grace Course*. Begin it on the day you attend the first session of *The Grace Course* and you'll receive concise, relevant, thought-provoking messages each day for eight weeks.

Available on The Bible App from YouVersion—search for "Daily Nuggets Of Grace." There is currently no charge for this.

THE GRACE CONNECTION BY STEVE GOSS

Steve Goss, author of *The Grace Course*, has written this book specifically for participants on the course. It fleshes out the principles taught on the course to help you connect with grace at a deeper level than ever before.

Published by Freedom In Christ Ministries International. Kindle version available.

THE WONDER OF GRACE: A 40-DAY DEVOTIONAL JOURNEY BY RICH MILLER

A revised and updated version of *40 Days Of Grace*, the 40-day devotional book by Rich Miller that has been so popular with participants on the original *Grace Course*. It is designed to be used directly after *The Grace Course* for a six-week period and will help participants process the principles they learned and put them into practice.

Published by Freedom In Christ Ministries International. Gift edition published by Christian Art Gifts.

MEET THE VIDEO PRESENTERS

Leisha Lyn-Cook lives in Kingston, Jamaica, and is an entrepreneur in the baking and pastry industry. Her business produces the most amazing cakes! She serves as a Small Group Facilitator and member of the missions ministry in her church and has also worked in youth ministry. She loves to participate in short-term missions with Operation Mobilization and managed to squeeze in a mission trip to Greece on her way to filming *The Grace Course*. She is part of the Freedom In Christ Jamaica team, and her greatest desire is to impact the world for Christ and to see lives truly changed through the transformative power of the Holy Spirit.

Josh Shaarda came to know Christ as a young child and went on to study at Bible College. However, having made some bad choices, he was filled with shame and guilt, and hated himself. He had a revelation of how complete God's unconditional love and forgiveness are and offered himself afresh in gratitude to serve him. Soon after, he met Mandy, who became his wife (they have five children), and they set off to share God with an unreached tribe in a remote part of Nigeria. They have now served in Africa for 21 years. Currently based in rural Uganda, Josh leads Freedom In Christ Uganda and for the past 12 years has been using the Freedom In Christ discipleship materials in villages and prisons with great results.

Nancy Maldonado was born in the Andes mountains of Ecuador, where she built forts and caught tadpoles with Rob, her childhood friend. They went on to marry and lived many adventures as missionaries in Spain, but their greatest adventure was parenting Josue and Sofia in a postmodern secular society. Nancy is part of Freedom In Christ's international team and is responsible for translating discipleship resources into Spanish. She loves trying new recipes, discipling women, bright colors, and Earl Grey tea with milk. She spends much of her time traveling around South and Central America with Rob, who is Freedom In Christ's Latin America Director. Nancy is one of the presenters of *The Freedom In Christ Course* and is much loved by viewers of it.

Rob Davies is married to Katharine and has three children and a very large and hairy dog. He loves the great outdoors. He's been Freedom In Christ UK's Executive Director since 2016 and prior to that was a missionary to Uganda. Through many adventures on the mission field and at home he's learning—more often than not the hard way—to trust that God's grace is always sufficient for life, leadership, and possibly most pertinently, for parenting. He's passionate about seeing people from all walks of life—every generation and every nation—embrace the freedom Jesus has won for them, and step into all God has prepared in advance for them.

Sidhara Udalagama grew up in Sri Lanka but has spent her adult years in England working in full-time ministry after graduating with a masters in organizational psychology. She currently works at a global not-for-profit organization as a communications specialist and speaker.

Alongside working in ministry, Sidhara has worked with corporate and not-for-profit organizations as a leadership development coach involved in staff training and the development of organizational–health focused content. She is a prolific communicator of the Bible with a passion to see people fulfill their potential in this world and become all that God created them to be.

Sidhara is married to Dev and enjoys eating, traveling the world, and repeating those two things . . . preferably together!

FREEDOM
IN CHRIST

session **01**

FREE!

OBJECTIVE

To understand that what really matters to God is not only *what* we do but *why* we do it.

FOCUS VERSE

We love because he first loved us.

1 John 4:19

 ### FOCUS TRUTH

In Christ we are perfectly loved and accepted for who we are, not what we do. From that position of security, we can make a free choice to serve God because we love Him, and get rid of any other false motivation.

 ### CONNECT

One definition of grace is "getting what you don't deserve." Tell the group about a time you got what you didn't deserve. What did you deserve? What did you actually get?

If you watched *The Wonder Of Grace* introductory video for this session, what was the main thing that struck you?

PRAYER & DECLARATION

Dear Father God, thank You for adopting us as Your children through Jesus Christ, and for giving us the privilege of calling You "Abba, Father"! As I begin this journey of knowing You more and understanding Your amazing grace, I submit to You so that Your truth will become true not just in my head, but in my heart. Amen.

I HAVE BEEN SET FREE BY THE BLOOD OF JESUS. I CHOOSE TO SUBMIT MYSELF TO GOD, AND I RESIST ANYTHING AND EVERYTHING THAT WOULD TRY TO COMPROMISE MY FREEDOM IN HIM.

WORD

THE STORY OF THE TWO BROTHERS—LUKE 15:11–32

Jesus said that He came to give us life in all its fullness. And He meant it. He wants to do amazing things in you and through you.

The Grace Course is designed to help you experience God's amazing grace like never before so that you can be more fruitful in God's Kingdom than perhaps you ever imagined.

We're going to explore the barriers to experiencing grace in our lives and how to remove them.

> THE YOUNGER BROTHER

Jesus deliberately paints a picture of the worst behavior imaginable in the culture of that time. The younger brother showed no respect for his father. He slept around. He took a job looking after pigs.

Out of desperation he returns home knowing he has blown any chance of being received back as a son and hoping he might possibly get paid work.

He expects—and deserves—to be dis-owned or at best severely punished.

But instead his father throws a magnifi-cent banquet and gives him three very significant things:

The robe would have been the best robe in the house, perhaps the father's own robe. It says clearly that the son had once again been given the right to enjoy the place of "right standing" with the father.

The ring enabled the son to make the father's official mark on documents to authorize expenditure. He had squan-dered his father's wealth, but the father gives him free access to the bank account.

The sandals: only the father and the sons were allowed footwear in the home. The father is declaring that this boy is still his son and is completely restored to the family.

> TWO SCENES FROM THE STORY

Scene 1: The younger son at the point that he collapses into his father's arms and casts himself on his mercy. He stands there dirty, smelly, broken. Acutely aware of his failure. Deeply ashamed of what he has become. He can scarcely believe it as it dawns upon him that his father still loves him, that he is forgiven and will not be punished.

Most of us get stuck in this first scene. We know we're forgiven and loved by God. But perhaps we still feel that we're essentially the same no-good failures we always were.

It's as if our understanding of the Gospel has got as far as Good Friday: Jesus died to forgive my sins and I'm going to go to heaven when I die. But right now? Well, I may be forgiven. But I'm still the same no-good let-down to God I always was.

Scene 2: Just minutes later the son is standing there, dressed in the finest robe, with the father's ring on his finger and sandals on his feet, feasting on the finest food. He is acutely aware of his past failures and knows he does not deserve all this. But it is dawning on him that he has not just been forgiven. He has also been completely restored to his former position, with free access to everything his father owns.

Which of these two scenes most accurately represents how you see yourself in relation to God right now?

We make it through to the second scene when we understand that Easter Sunday is not just to celebrate the fact that Jesus rose from the dead but also celebrates the fact that we rose from the dead with Him and became someone completely new at the deepest level of our being.

If you know Jesus, you are completely restored right now. Deep down inside you are a totally new person. And God doesn't just love you. He absolutely delights in you.

THE FATHER IS WAITING FOR YOU

If you have never responded to Jesus and do not yet know Him, Father God is waiting for you. No matter what you've done or what has been done to you, you can respond to Him in your heart and choose to accept His free gift of salvation.

> THE OLDER BROTHER

Jesus looked like a religious teacher, but He didn't behave the way the religious people expected Him to. In particular, He mixed with the "wrong" crowd, and they were saying, "This man welcomes sinners and even sits down to eat with them" (see Luke 15:2).

This story is part of Jesus' response, and the elder brother is clearly meant to represent these religious people.

He had not turned away from his father and thrown everything back in his face. He had stayed and worked hard. He had done what was expected of him.

His motivation was the inheritance that he would one day receive in return for "slaving away" day after day. To him, it was clearly a transaction: you earn the father's favor by what you do.

The father's love and acceptance had as little to do with his good outward behavior as it did with the younger son's bad outward behavior.

God's love, acceptance, and favor have nothing to do with our behavior, good or bad. But everything to do with His grace.

Instead of working in the fields for years, the older brother could have been enjoying everything the father had. What a tragedy to go through life slaving away to try to earn something that in fact you already have.

We can be like him. We do not know what we already have or who we are in Christ. On one level we know we are saved by grace, not by obeying rules. But we slip into thinking that being a disciple of Jesus means somehow having to maintain that favor by doing the right things.

Jesus' story makes clear that God's acceptance of us, today, tomorrow, and every day after that, does not depend on what we do or fail to do. It depends solely on His grace.

God does not want us to fail but He gives us freedom to fail. However, even if we fall flat on our face and make a complete mess, God will pick us up, dust us off, and welcome us back.

PAUSE FOR THOUGHT 2

1. The younger brother has been received back as a son, but the elder brother refuses to go into the house with the father, preferring to remain in the fields acting like a slave. Why do you think he does that? Which son do you identify with more?

2. If you knew for sure that God's acceptance of you and love for you did not depend on how well you behaved, how might that change the way you live?

> SLAVING OR SERVING?

Some of us are sidetracked by the world out there and its false promises and become like the younger brother.

The younger son went to a "distant land," whereas the elder brother stayed at home. But in the story we do not find him in the home with the father. Instead he is out in the fields "slaving away."

The younger son hoped that he might become a hired servant and earn anything that came from the father. But the older son had beaten him to it and had assumed the identity of a hired servant.

Both walked away from their true identity as sons. Both removed themselves from their relationship with their father.

Both ended up thinking they had to earn the father's favor.

At the start of our Christian life, most of us identify strongly with the younger son. We know we need forgiveness and salvation and are so grateful to receive them.

At that point we begin a new relationship with our Heavenly Father. And the idea is that we begin a journey of knowing Him and becoming more and more like Him.

But some of us are sidetracked by the world out there and its false promises and become like the younger brother.

Others are sidetracked by religious rules and become like the elder brother, thinking that being a Christian is about doing the "right" things.

But when discipleship becomes just obeying rules, the Christian life is a joyless trudge. It's supposed to work the other way around.

As the younger son returns to his old duties, he knows that, even if he chooses not to do them, the father will still love him and he will still be his son.

Knowing what he now knows about the father and out of this incredible new relationship with him, won't he choose to do them and do them well, not because he *has* to but because he *wants* to, not to earn anything but purely out of love?

> WHAT WE DO MATTERS

A day will come at the end of the age when God will test what we have done to see if it has any real value.

Paul tells us that a day will come at the end of the age when God tests what we've done to see if it has any real value (1 Corinthians 3:12–15).

He uses the analogy of a building that's on fire and says that the fire will burn up the things that are of no value—"wood, hay, straw"—while things we do that are of value—"gold, silver, precious stones"—will remain forever.

Jesus tells us that some will come to Him at the end of time and say they did amazing things like driving out demons and performing miracles in His name. Are those wood, hay, and straw or gold, silver, and precious stones? Well, Jesus says He will say to them, "I never knew you. Away from me, you evildoers!" (Matthew 7:22–23).

> IT'S NOT JUST WHAT WE DO BUT WHY WE DO IT

Two people can do the same thing. One will delight God and count for eternity; the other will not.

What's the difference?

"If I give away all I have, and if I deliver up my body to be burned, but have not love, I gain nothing" (1 Corinthians 13:3).

If our motivation is not love, then no matter how good our actions look, they are worth precisely nothing. They are wood, hay, and straw. What is important to God is not just what we do but why we do it.

When God chose an unlikely candidate, David, to be king of Israel, Samuel said, "The LORD sees not as man sees: man looks on the outward appearance, but the LORD looks on the heart" (1 Samuel 16:7).

When Jesus said, "If you love me, you will keep my commandments" (John 14:15), He was simply explaining a fact. If I love Him, I will obey His commands. I just will.

"We love because he first loved us" (1 John 4:19). When we know how much He loves us, we will love Him back. We just will. We will find ourselves doing the things that please Him automatically, not out of obligation.

That is why understanding grace is crucial. Then we can be like Paul, who said it's "Christ's love [that] compels us" (2 Corinthians 5:14 NIV).

God wants our motivation to be love and nothing but love.

The Grace Course will give you the opportunity to root out "false motivators" such as shame, guilt, fear, pride, or the need to perform and please others.

> THE FATHER

The Father is looking out for you, whether you are in full rebellion or slaving away in the fields. When He sees you, He will run out and embrace you—and call for the robe, the ring, and the sandals. Will you put them on?

When He tells you that all He has is already yours—His whole, vast, rich estate—will you come back inside the house and enjoy it with Him?

From that position of love and security, will you do the things He has prepared for you to do, not because you have to, but just because you love Him?

Will you make Jesus not just your Savior, but your King?

REFLECT

Think about what you are doing to serve God across the whole of your life. Are these things motivated by your love for God or by other things?

Ask God to help you understand what needs to change so that your motivation becomes love and nothing but love.

Why do you think that God puts so much importance on your motivation being love?

session **02**

UNASHAMED!

OBJECTIVE

To understand that our very identity at the core of our being was comprehensively transformed the moment we came to Christ.

FOCUS VERSE

For our sake he made him to be sin who knew no sin, so that in him we might become the righteousness of God.

2 Corinthians 5:21

FOCUS TRUTH

We have not just been covered with the righteousness of Christ. We have actually become the righteousness of God.

CONNECT

Tell the group about an embarrassing moment you have experienced.

Divide into pairs and take turns reading Hebrews 10:19–22 out loud to each other, inserting the other person's name:

> "Therefore, _____ (their name), since you have confidence to enter the Most Holy Place by the blood of Jesus," etc.

If you watched *The Wonder Of Grace* introductory video for this session, what was the main thing that struck you?

Was there anything in the YouVersion "Daily Nuggets Of Grace" that especially made you think?

PRAYER & DECLARATION

Heavenly Father, we welcome Your presence with us right now. Please continue to root out any "false motivators" within us so that it's love for Jesus alone that drives us on as Your children. Please teach us today how Your grace brings us out of disgrace into freedom. Amen.

I DECLARE THE TRUTH THAT I AM NOW A NEW CREATION IN CHRIST; THE OLD HAS GONE AND THE NEW HAS COME! I HAVE BEEN CLEANSED FROM SIN AND NO LONGER HAVE TO HIDE BEHIND MASKS. I COMMAND EVERY ENEMY OF THE LORD JESUS TO LEAVE MY PRESENCE.

WORD

The Grace Course will help us root out "false motivators" and make sure that it's love for Jesus—and nothing but love for Jesus—that drives us on in our Christian life.

In this session we consider shame and in the next session we will look at guilt.

Guilt is about what we *do*. But shame is about who we *are*.

Guilt says, "I've *done* something wrong. I *made* a mistake." Shame, on the other hand, says, "There's something wrong with *me*." "*I am* the mistake." It strikes at our very identity.

> CONSEQUENCES OF ADAM AND EVE'S SIN

At the beginning of time, God's love moved Him to create incredible universes, amazing galaxies, and this wonderful planet.

The Father, the Son, and the Holy Spirit already enjoyed a beautiful, loving relationship, and God's great desire was to include others in that.

He created human beings and gave us a task: to work with Him to continue bringing order out of chaos, as we look after this world.

God didn't make us as robots who had to do what He told us to. Out of love, He gave us the ability to decide for ourselves.

God did not burden Adam and Eve with rules but said just one thing. He told them not to eat fruit from a certain tree, "for when you eat from it you will certainly die" (Genesis 2:17).

Genuine freedom includes genuine consequences for the choices we make. Out of love, God wanted Adam and Eve to avoid the unpleasant consequences of a bad choice.

God's enemy, Satan, deceived Eve. She and Adam chose to disobey God and, as God had warned, there were huge consequences, not just for them but for their children, their children's children, and all their descendants.

Adam and Eve died spiritually. They lost their spiritual connection to God and all that came with it: their significance, their intimacy with God, their security.

Their fundamental identity changed. Paul says, "by the one man's disobedience the many were made sinners" (Romans 5:19).

> WHAT IS A "SINNER?"

In the New Testament the word *sinner* describes those who are spiritually dead, who are disconnected from God. Being a sinner is a condition, a state of being.

We didn't *become* sinners the first time we sinned. It's the other way around. We were born spiritually dead—disconnected, cut off from the life of God—and therefore our default setting was to sin.

> SHAME MAKES US WANT TO HIDE

Before Adam sinned, Genesis tells us, "The man and his wife were both naked and were not ashamed" (Genesis 2:25).

But afterwards, "The eyes of both of them were opened, and they realized they were naked; so they sewed fig leaves together and made coverings for themselves" (Genesis 3:7 NIV).

Shame makes us feel so vulnerable that we want to cover up and hide away from God and other people.

Shame is to do with our identity. And, as we shall see, God's remedy is to give us a whole new identity.

PAUSE FOR THOUGHT 1

1. What has God done for you personally out of love? How do those things affect how you view yourself?

2. When we feel shame, we try to "cover up" and hide away like Adam and Eve did. What are some ways you have seen shame lead people to do that?

> SHAME IS INTENSIFIED BY SHAME-BASED CULTURES

Our life experiences tend to determine how much of an issue shame is for us. It's worse if we were raised in a shame-based culture.

All societies have ways of making us conform to their expectations. Anthropologists will tell you that individualistic Western societies tend to use *guilt* for this, and we'll look at that in the next session.

Other societies, particularly Eastern and African ones, use *shame*. In these more collectivistic cultures, if you don't conform to social norms, you bring dishonor and shame to yourself and to your family.

In a shame-based culture what matters most is obtaining honor and avoiding shame, being accepted and avoiding rejection by the community. It's not so much a question of whether what you do is wrong or right but whether it meets the expectations of the group.

Some institutions—even Christian ones, or perhaps *especially* Christian ones—can create shame-based subcultures, even in a society that is not shame-based.

And *parents* can unwittingly create a culture of particular expectations. If children feel they don't measure up, it can be devastating.

The world also sets unreachable standards, for example about the way we look. If we believe the world's lies about beauty, we end up feeling ugly, like there's something wrong with **us**. So we try to "fix" our appearance to fit in and be accepted.

> SHAME IS INTENSIFIED BY PAST EXPERIENCES

We can also be predisposed to feel shame because of things we've done. Or things other people did to us, particularly in childhood.

Maybe we were abused in some way. Maybe we even feel it was somehow our fault or that we deserved it. But children are never to blame for the shameful acts of perpetrators.

> THE "LESS MESS"

> *Shame's basic message is that there's something wrong with* **us**, *that* **we** *are the problem.*

Shame's basic message is that there's something wrong with **us**, that **we** are the problem. It puts us into "the less mess." We feel help*less*, worth*less*, mean-ing*less*, power*less*, hope*less*.

So we hide, we wear masks, we avoid, we pretend. Other defense mechanisms include:

- Lying
- Blame-shifting
- Pretending everything is fine
- Criticizing others in order to make them appear inferior to us

- Compromising moral or biblical values to fit in
- Self-medicating in order to numb the pain of our shame
- Striving for perfection

All of these things are like Adam and Eve's fig leaves: they don't work to cover our shame. They may offer some relief, but in the end, like all strategies of the flesh, they fail. God has a better way!

PAUSE FOR THOUGHT 2

1. **Has any person or any culture you have experienced used shame to try to make you behave in a certain way? How has it affected you?**

2. **What would God say to you about situations where you felt shame?**

> THE GREAT EXCHANGE

Shame strikes at our very identity.

Shame strikes at our very identity.

The younger brother no longer saw himself as a son but had taken on the identity of a servant—someone who would be accepted only based on performance.

OUR OLD IDENTITY

We were all born spiritually dead—disconnected from God.

We were "by nature children of wrath" (Ephesians 2:3).

We were not the people God intended us to be, and there was nothing we could do about it.

OUR NEW IDENTITY

"While we *were* still sinners, Christ died for us" (Romans 5:8).

The New Testament uses the word *sinner* to describe those who are not Christians. This verse makes clear that that's not who we are any more.

"For our sake he made him to *be* sin who knew no sin, so that in him we might *become* the righteousness of God." (2 Corinthians 5:21)

On the cross, Jesus, who was totally blameless, *became* sin for our sake. God took all our shortcomings, failures, rebellion, and shame—and laid them on Christ. He didn't die just to pay the penalty for our sin. He took on Himself our defiled, unclean nature and destroyed our inner contamination.

When we surrender our life to Jesus, a great exchange takes place. We don't just get our sins forgiven. We *become* the righteousness of God.

Ezekiel's prophecy is fulfilled: we get a new heart and a new spirit (Ezekiel 11:19).

We are no longer *by nature* children of wrath because we now share God's *divine nature* (2 Peter 1:4).

When Jesus rose from the dead to new life, we rose with Him. We have become a whole new person. We now have a totally new, clean, wonderful identity.

The Bible no longer calls us "sinners." Its standard word for those who are in Christ is "holy ones." *Holy* means set apart for God. Special.

Deep in the core of your being, your very identity has changed. From someone disconnected, cut off from God, to someone who is accepted, significant, and secure in Christ.

Your shame has been completely taken away. Once and for all. Past, present, and future! You're not contaminated any more. You're not unacceptable. You're clean. You're presentable. You can take off your mask and let down the walls. You can show yourself to God and to others with no shame whatsoever!

Here's God's invitation to you:

> Since we have confidence to enter the holy places by the blood of Jesus, by the new and living way that he opened for us through the curtain, that is, through his flesh, and since we have a great priest over the house of God, let us draw near with a true heart in full assurance of faith, with our hearts sprinkled clean from an evil conscience and our bodies washed with pure water. (Hebrews 10:19–22)

We don't have to run away anymore. We don't have to hide, no matter what's in our past, or even in our present, because we have a new, clean identity in Christ. We're invited to come near to God in the Holy of Holies—because we *are* holy ones!

> OUR NEW NAME

"The nations shall see your righteousness, and all the kings your glory, and you shall be called by a new name that the mouth of the LORD will give." (Isaiah 62:2)

God has given you a new name—many new names (see pages 30–31).

In the Bible, names were much more than labels. They were seen as a reflection of a person's identity. These new names are truths about you at the deepest level of your being.

The question we all face is: Am I going to believe what God says about me in His Word? Or am I going to believe what my past experiences, my present struggles, or other people tell me?

Let's allow God's grace to bring us out of disgrace and learn to live as the holy ones we are!

REFLECT

Write down the "new name(s)" that particularly strike a chord with you. Thank God for who you now are.

Sharing with someone else helps to move this truth from the head to the heart. At an appropriate moment, turn to your neighbor and share with each other your new names. Who else can you share your new name with in the coming week?

> MY NEW NAME

My new name is **Beloved** (Colossians 3:12)

My new name is **Chosen** (Ephesians 1:4)

My new name is **Precious** (Isaiah 43:4)

My new name is **Loved** (1 John 4:10)

My new name is **Clean** (John 15:3)

My new name is **Presentable** (Luke 17:14)

My new name is **Protected** (Psalm 91:14, John 17:15)

My new name is **Welcomed** (Ephesians 3:12)

My new name is **Heir** (Romans 8:17, Galatians 3:29)

My new name is **Complete** (Colossians 2:10)

My new name is **Holy** (Hebrews 10:10, Ephesians 1:4)

My new name is **Forgiven** (Psalm 103:3, Colossians 2:13)

My new name is **Adopted** (Ephesians 1:5)

My new name is **Delight** (Psalm 147:11)

My new name is **Unashamed** (Romans 10:11)

My new name is **Known** (Psalm 139:1)

My new name is **Planned** (Ephesians 1:11–12)

My new name is **Gifted** (2 Timothy 1:6, 1 Corinthians 12:11)

My new name is **Enriched** (2 Corinthians 8:9)

My new name is **Provided For** (1 Timothy 6:17)

My new name is **Treasured** (Deuteronomy 7:6)

My new name is **Pure** (1 Corinthians 6:11)

My new name is **Established** (Romans 16:25)

My new name is **God's Work of Art** (Ephesians 2:10)

My new name is **Helped** (Hebrews 13:5)

My new name is **Free from Condemnation** (Romans 8:1)

My new name is **God's Child** (Romans 8:15)

My new name is **Christ's Friend** (John 15:15)

My new name is **Christ's Precious Bride** (Isaiah 54:5, Song of Songs 7:10)

session **03**

INNOCENT!

OBJECTIVE

To understand that our guilt before God was completely dealt with at the cross, that any guilt feelings that remain are not based on reality, and that God uses grace rather than guilt to motivate us to live a holy life.

FOCUS VERSE

"And when you were dead in your wrongdoings and the uncircumcision of your flesh, He made you alive together with Him, having forgiven us all our wrongdoings, having canceled the certificate of debt consisting of decrees against us, which was hostile to us; and He has taken it out of the way, having nailed it to the cross."

Colossians 2:13–14 NASB

 FOCUS TRUTH

No matter what we have done (even as Christians) and no matter how guilty we may feel, the truth is that our guilt has been completely and utterly paid for by Christ's death on the cross so that we can stand confidently before God, who is pure and holy.

 CONNECT

Which road sign would best describe where you are on your journey with God right now? (e.g., stop, steep gradient, detour, crossroads).

How do you think God would introduce you to me based on your new identity? (For ideas, look back at your new names at the end of session 2.)

If you watched *The Wonder Of Grace* introductory video for this session, what was the main thing that struck you?

Was there anything in the YouVersion "Daily Nuggets Of Grace" that especially made you think?

Heavenly Father, thank You that because I have chosen to make Jesus my King, I have received His free gift of life. Thank You that, in Him, all of Your expectations of me are met in full, meaning I don't need to try harder, prove anything, or compare myself to others. Please help me understand that, even when I go wrong, Jesus' full and complete sacrifice for me remains effective. I'm still forgiven. My guilt is gone. Forever. Amen.

IN CHRIST, I AM FORGIVEN AND DECLARED INNOCENT OF ALL THE CHARGES THAT WERE STACKED AGAINST ME. SO BY THE AUTHORITY OF THE LORD JESUS CHRIST I COMMAND ANY ACCUSING AND CONDEMNING THOUGHTS IN MY MIND TO GO NOW.

WORD

HOLY ONES

How do you feel about the Bible identifying you as a "holy one" rather than a "sinner"?

Would it be better to continue to identify ourselves as sinners because it is real and honest and might keep us humble, aware of our weakness, and less likely to sin again?

Well, what do sinners do, by definition? They sin! To have any hope of living a godly life as a disciple of Jesus, we have to know the truth that we are holy ones.

> GOD AND GUILT

What if you were asked to write the ending to the story of the two brothers starting at the point where the younger brother returns home and asks the father to receive him back as a hired laborer—would you portray the father differently than the way Jesus did?

Shouldn't the father expect the son to be thorough in his apology? Shouldn't the son be made aware of how he offended the father and abandoned the family? Shouldn't the son have to prove himself for a time to earn trust and only then be allowed to spend money again?

Your response will depend on how you see God.

Some of us worry, *I don't pray enough; I failed to read the Bible in one year; I'm a flop at sharing my faith; I don't have the spiritual gifts she does; I don't seem to hear from God like him; I'm not fruitful;* or any number of other things.

We feel God shakes His head in disappointment and disapproval, and we just want to hide from Him.

We either walk away, forever resolve to try harder tomorrow, or just resign ourselves to remaining a second-class Christian. That's not how God wants us to live.

> WHY JESUS CAME

Why did God send Jesus, His only Son, to die for us?

Most of us have learned to respond by saying, "to forgive my sins." And that is true. But consider three specific reasons Jesus Himself gave:

> **"For the Son of Man came . . . to seek and to save the lost."**
> **(Luke 19:10 NIV)**

God is love. In His love, God was moved to pursue and rescue us who were lost. Not to have us burn ourselves out trying to please Him.

> **"I have come . . . that they may have life, and have it to the full."**
> **(John 10:10 NIV)**

Adam lost life. Jesus came specifically to give that life back.

"The Son of Man did not come to be served, but to serve, and to give his life as a ransom for many." (Matthew 20:28 NIV)

A ransom is what was paid to buy someone out of slavery. Jesus gave His life to buy you out of slavery to death, to the flesh, to sin, and to Satan.

In three different verses where Jesus explains why He came, He doesn't even mention that He came to forgive our sins (though He did do that too).

Here are the verses most used in our Gospel presentations:

"For God so loved the world that he gave his one and only Son, that whoever believes in him shall not perish but have eternal life. For God did not send his Son into the world to condemn the world, but to save the world through him." (John 3:16–17 NIV)

Again, there is no mention of sins or guilt or forgiveness. It's about *life*.

We *were* guilty and Jesus *did* die to forgive our sins. The point we are making is that, when Jesus and Paul and the biblical writers explained the good news, guilt and forgiveness were not the focus of their explanations.

> THE CHURCH'S HISTORIC FOCUS ON GUILT

We tend to focus on guilt more than other aspects of the Gospel message, largely for historic and cultural reasons.

In many "Christian" countries, the Church acted as a kind of police officer for the state. For centuries it focused on guilt and punishment and warned the populace that God was watching our behavior closely and keeping tabs on us.

Earning our way into God's good books by our behavior took center stage in our understanding of God and the Gospel.

Even though we know on one level that we're saved by grace alone through faith, when it comes to living as disciples day by day, many of us are followed around by that cloud of guilt or that nagging feeling that we're not doing enough or not doing it quite right.

We have learned to see God as a nit-picking, strict, and hard-to-please grouch, and to those outside we can come across as a bunch of kill-joys focused on sin, condemnation, and judgment.

PAUSE FOR THOUGHT 1

1. Has any person or any culture you have experienced used guilt to try to make you behave in a certain way? How has it affected you?

2. In what ways do the reasons Jesus gave for His coming—"Life," "Saved," and "Ransomed"—give you a bigger perspective? How would you explain succinctly to someone else why Jesus came?

> GOD IS LOVE

God is love. And His heart is not to condemn but to make things right.

In the Bible, when Adam sinned, the primary consequence of that sin was spiritual death.

God is not portrayed as an angry figure who feels wronged and so turns His back on the people He created. No, He provided clothes for Adam and Eve and immediately put into motion a plan to restore humanity, even though He knew it would lead to the death of His Son.

God is love. And His heart is not to condemn but to make things right.

> FACT NOT FEELING

Are you guilty before God?

Guilt is a legal concept used in the context of a courtroom. A judge or jury, after hearing the facts of the case, comes to a decision that the charge against the defendant is true and pronounces that person guilty. Guilt is a fact, not a feeling.

In our laws, guilt often leads to a financial penalty. The concepts of guilt and debt are strongly associated. When you say the Lord's Prayer, you may say, "Forgive us our sins (or trespasses)," but the Greek word's core meaning is "debts."

In New Testament times, if someone borrowed money from someone else, a legal document was drawn up itemizing exactly what was owed to whom, what the repayment terms were, and what the consequences for default would be. It was called a certificate of debt.

If someone couldn't repay the debt, their property was seized and sold, or they themselves could be taken into slavery.

"And when you were dead in your wrongdoings and the uncircumcision of your flesh, He made you alive together with Him, having forgiven us all our wrongdoings, having canceled the certificate of debt consisting of decrees against us, which was hostile to us; and He has taken it out of the way, having nailed it to the cross" (Colossians 2:13–14 NASB).

The USA has a national debt of around 33 trillion dollars and a population of around 330 million. That's a debt of $100,000 for every American citizen. Imagine a baby born today. Through no fault of its own but just by being born American and because of the spending of previous generations, it immediately has a debt of $100,000!

Because of Adam's rebellion, we were all born with a certificate of debt to God. That is to say, we were guilty before God even as we took our first breath. Our subsequent sins increased that debt. And we had no way to pay it.

These verses tell us that God did two significant things. First, He made us *alive* with Christ and gave us that incredible new identity. Then God wrote *"paid in full"* across our certificate of debt, which He nailed to the cross with Jesus.

We have no guilt whatsoever. We are totally debt free!

All of our sins have been forgiven—past, present, and future.

We have no guilt whatsoever. We are totally debt free!

"There is therefore now no condemnation for those who are in Christ Jesus" (Romans 8:1).

Now means now and no means no!

The best a human court can do is declare us "not guilty." God's grace goes further than that. As far as God is concerned, it's as if what you and I did never took place. He declares us "innocent"! And that's a legal fact.

In Christ, all of God's expectations of you have been met in full. You don't need to try harder or compare yourself to others. You have nothing to prove, no debt to pay off. Your guilt is gone. Forever. You are innocent! It's a fact!

And if you still *feel* guilty? Then your feelings are lying to you.

Either your conscience has not yet fully grasped the wonder of Christ's total forgiveness, or you are listening to the lies of your enemy, Satan. In either case, the answer is to make a choice to believe that what God tells you clearly in His Word is true. You are innocent!

PAUSE FOR THOUGHT 2

1. Can you think of a time when you or someone else did something wrong but did not feel guilty or, conversely, felt guilty for something that was not actually wrong?

2. Share with the group what the word *debt* brings to mind. Have you ever had a debt you could not pay?

3. What do you feel about being declared "innocent" by God Himself?

> CAN WE KEEP ON SINNING?

If God accepts us back with no questions asked, can we just do whatever we like?

In the letter to the seven churches in Revelation, there is just one, the church in Thyatira, that is commended for its love. But they seem to think that grace means you can do whatever you like, and they are allowing sexual immorality and idol worship. Jesus' words about the consequences of this, for the ringleader, make for uncomfortable reading:

> "Behold, I will throw her onto a sickbed, and those who commit adultery with her I will throw into great tribulation, unless they repent of her works, and I will strike her children dead." (Revelation 2:22–23)

Perhaps you find it hard to accept that Jesus would use this kind of language. But God is love. Therefore, everything He does, and everything He says, must come from love.

Out of love God has laid down boundaries in order to *protect* us. He told Adam not to eat from the tree because He knew the consequences. And it's because God *loves* this lady and this church that He tells her not to continue sinning. His intent is that they will *not* suffer, will *not* die. When we truly understand the consequences of sin, we'll also understand why God takes it so seriously.

If we see a child moving along a branch that we know is going to break, we may start shouting and running toward them. To the child we will appear angry, but in fact we are expressing love.

> This is the message we have heard from him and proclaim to you, that God is light, and in him is no darkness at all. If we say we have fellowship with him while we walk in darkness, we lie and do not practice the truth. But if we walk in the light, as he is in the light, we have fellowship with one another, and the blood of Jesus his Son cleanses us from all sin. If we say we have no sin, we deceive ourselves, and the truth is not in us. If we confess our sins, he is faithful and just to forgive us our sins and to cleanse us from all unrighteousness. (1 John 1:5–9)

If we are walking openly with our Father, we will *want* to live in the light. If someone persists in sin and is not bothered by it, there would be a serious question about whether they actually know Jesus at all.

> WHEN WE GO WRONG

For those of us who know Jesus, our flesh will relentlessly pull us toward sin. If we say we do not ever fall for it, we are deceiving ourselves.

However, when we know that God is not angry with us, but still loves us just as much as before, we can agree with Him that we have sinned—that's what "confessing" means—but we can also agree with Him that we are completely forgiven in Christ.

"Submit yourselves therefore to God. Resist the devil, and he will flee from you" (James 4:7).

Confession is part of what James calls submitting to God, but he tells us also to "resist the devil." The biggest issue with sin is that it opens a door of influence to the enemy in our lives that will stop us from being fruitful. We need to close that door by submitting *and* resisting.

The Steps To Freedom In Christ is a kind, gentle way to do this.

The Steps To Experiencing God's Grace, which comes at the end of this course, is a similar process where you will deal with barriers to grace in your life.

When we respond in repentance, God cleanses us from *all* evil and unrighteousness and restores us to fellowship with Jesus and with others.

> GOD DOES NOT WANT US TO FEEL GUILTY

Is there any place for using guilt as a motivator, perhaps to encourage people not to sin?

There were a lot of sin issues in the Corinthian church: jealousy, quarreling, sexual immorality, drunkenness, and class discrimination to name but a few.

Paul did not overlook them but agonized over how to address them because he understood the serious consequences of sin. He decided to write them a tough letter. The strategy worked, and in a subsequent letter he said this:

> I . . . rejoice, not that you were made sorrowful, but that you were made sorrowful to the point of repentance. . . . For the sorrow that is according to the will of God produces a repentance without regret, leading to salvation, but the sorrow of the world produces death. (2 Corinthians 7:9–10 NASB)

WORLDLY SORROW

After Judas betrayed Jesus, he was filled with remorse but had no hope. Instead of trusting in the One who was going to the cross for him, he turned away and hanged himself.

The way many of us have learned to respond to sin in our lives is through a self-destructive cycle of sin and guilt. This is worldly sorrow.

GODLY SORROW

Paul's aim was not to make the Corinthians feel guilty and respond with worldly sorrow. He wanted them to experience godly sorrow that would lead to "repentance without regret."

Peter had betrayed his best friend in His greatest hour of need by denying Him three times. When Jesus catches up with him after His resurrection, He doesn't even mention this monumental failure. He cooks him breakfast and asks him gently three times if he loves Him—once for each of his previous denials. Then Jesus restores him. And this grace meant that Peter was able to experience godly sorrow and could move forward.

God wants us to understand that all sin has consequences, but He doesn't want us to be weighed down with guilt, no matter what we have done or what we are caught in right now. He wants that sense of godly sorrow to pull us into His arms, where we will find the same welcome the younger son received.

> GRACE—THE MOST POWERFUL MOTIVATOR

So *can* you do whatever you want? If you are still asking that question, you are missing the point. When you truly "get" grace, you will not want to keep sinning.

It is grace, not guilt, that is the most powerful motivator to live a righteous life.

REFLECT

Ask God to show you things that you have experienced that have caused you to doubt that He is love. Write them down. Bring them to Him in prayer. Then ask Him to help you begin to understand how He has remained true to His fundamental character of love in those situations.

session **04**

VICTORIOUS!

OBJECTIVE

To help us understand why our new identity in Christ means that, even though we will sin from time to time, at any given moment we can choose not to, and we can put an end to sin-confess cycles.

FOCUS VERSE

"For one who has died has been set free from sin."

Romans 6:7

 ## FOCUS TRUTH

We need to learn to take the whole of reality into account (including the unseen spiritual world) in order to experience the breaking of the power of sin in our lives. But, through God's grace, we genuinely can live in victory over sin and Satan.

 ## CONNECT

Would you rather be a caterpillar or a butterfly? Why?

In Romans 8, Paul speaks to Christians who are facing tough things: he mentions trouble, hardship, persecution, famine, and the ever-present possibility of death. Then he says (verse 37): "In all these things we are more than conquerors through him who loved us."

How have you experienced knowing that you are "more than a conqueror" in Christ in the midst of difficult circumstances?

You might also like to consider what Paul says next:

> For I am convinced that neither death nor life, neither angels nor demons, neither the present nor the future, nor any powers, neither height nor depth, nor anything else in all creation, will be able to separate us from the love of God that is in Christ Jesus our Lord. (Romans 8:38–39 NIV).

If you watched *The Wonder Of Grace* introductory video for this session, what was the main thing that struck you?

Was there anything in the YouVersion "Daily Nuggets Of Grace" that especially made you think?

WORD

WHAT YOU *DO* COMES FROM WHO YOU *ARE*

Paul says that we are "more than conquerors" (Romans 8:37); we are victorious. In this session, we're going to think about the grace God gives us when we face temptation or when we feel caught in a sin and just don't seem to be able to escape.

We'll focus on a key principle: what you *do* comes from who you *are*.

Second Corinthians 5:17 is a dramatic statement about who we now are:

Therefore, if anyone is in Christ, he is a new creation. The old has passed away; behold, the new has come.

When we chose to follow Jesus, we became someone totally new. We're as different from how we were before as a butterfly is to a caterpillar. Deep down inside our nature is now clean and holy.

> FREE FROM THE POWER OF SIN

> For one who has died has been set free from sin. Now if we have died with Christ, we believe that we will also live with him. (Romans 6:7–8)

Most of us were taught to identify with Jesus in His death on Good Friday. His death dealt with the *penalty* of sin, and we received forgiveness for our sins because of His sacrifice.

But in Romans 6 Paul is not talking about *forgiveness* for sin. He is talking about being set free from *slavery* to sin, from the compulsion to sin.

And the key truth he wants us to know in order to deal with the *power* of sin is that we have risen to new life with Christ.

When someone you know dies, your relationship with them ends. Sin has not died—in fact it's very much still alive—but *we* have died with Christ, and that has ended our relationship with sin.

Paul's argument is that, just as Christ will never be subject to death again, because we have risen with Him, we need never be subject to slavery to sin again.

Have *you* died with Christ? Yes! Then you have been set free from sin.

You may very well be thinking "I don't *feel* free from sin. And sometimes I actually do sin."

Paul is well aware of this, so he now gives us three clear instructions based on these great truths. Here's the **first instruction**:

> So you also must consider yourselves dead to sin and alive to God in Christ Jesus. (Romans 6:11)

If you still see yourself as a sinner, even a forgiven sinner, what will you do? Sin! What you do comes from who you are, or who you think you are.

But we are much more than just forgiven:

We are alive again!

We are new creations!

We are the righteousness of God!

We are holy ones!

Paul's encouragement to us is to ignore our feelings and stick to the facts. Whatever we *feel*, the truth is that we *are* now alive to Christ and dead to sin. This is not something we need to strive to *make* true. It just *is* true. We simply need to make a choice to agree with God's Word and live accordingly.

Because you are a holy one who is risen with Christ to new life, at any given moment you are now genuinely free to make the right choice. What you *do* comes from who you *are*.

1. In John 8:31–32 Jesus says, "If you hold to my teaching . . . you will know the truth, and the truth will set you free" (NIV). He goes on to make clear that the freedom He is talking about is freedom from sin: "Very truly I tell you, everyone who sins is a slave to sin. Now a slave has no permanent place in the family, but a son belongs to it forever. So if the Son sets you free, you will be free indeed" (John 8:34–36 NIV). How does knowing the truth set us free from slavery to sin? What specific truth do we need to know?

2. How does the principle "What you do comes from who you are" change how you view the possibility of getting free from patterns of persistent sin in your life? What is your key takeaway from this principle?

> THE CONSEQUENCES OF BAD CHOICES

If a butterfly gets caught in the rain, it cannot fly and it ends up crawling slowly along the ground, acting just like a caterpillar.

Even though we are holy ones, we can act like sinners.

If we go wrong, God does not say to us, "You're a sinner!" His gentle words to us are more like this: "You're my child, you're a holy one, a whole new creation. You're *not* a sinner. So why are you *acting* like one?"

And when you, a holy one, act out of character and sin, it does not change who you are, or God's love for you. But it does affect your fruitfulness.

When we go wrong, we think the problem is that we have disappointed God, but Paul's **second instruction** demonstrates a quite different concern:

> Let not sin therefore reign in your mortal body, to make you obey its passions. (Romans 6:12)

Sin is like an "ex," and it *is* possible for us to rekindle our relationship with sin. Paul's concern is that we can end up hooked again—allowing sin to reign in Jesus' place and to turn us back into its slaves.

> SIN IS A SPIRITUAL WARFARE ISSUE

So how do we stop giving sin permission to reign in our bodies? Here's the **third instruction**:

> Do not present your members to sin as instruments for unrighteousness, but present yourselves to God as those who have been brought from death to life, and your members to God as instruments for righteousness. (Romans 6:13, emphasis added)

You can choose to use a car either to give someone in need a ride to church or to deal drugs. In the same way we have a choice as to how we use our bodies.

We can either present ourselves to sin or to God. There's no middle ground. Every day we make that choice.

This is not a battle just between us and our flesh. Paul talks about sin as if it's a person and makes clear (see Ephesians 4:26–27) that it is a spiritual warfare issue.

If we let the sun go down on our anger (which is not in itself a sin but just an emotion), we allow it to turn into the sin of unforgiveness and we give the devil a foothold—a place of influence—in our lives.

> OUR WORLDVIEW CAN GET IN THE WAY

If you've grown up in the West, you might acknowledge the existence of the devil and demons theologically, but our worldview predisposes us to ignore the reality of the spiritual world when it comes to living our daily lives. So even though we have the spiritual authority to deal with it, we end up getting duped into doing nothing, and our passivity means the devil keeps a foothold in our lives.

On the other hand, if you've grown up in a different culture, you might have a far greater awareness of the spiritual realm, but the chances are it's one rooted in fear that gives far too much power to the devil and the demonic. And you may think it's more complicated than simply submitting to God and resisting the devil (James 4:7). But it is not.

James 4:7 gives us two things to do: submit and resist.

> AN ANALOGY

Most Christians think that a sin issue is resolved by saying sorry to God and turning away from the sin, determining to do better. An analogy may help us understand why that isn't enough.

Suppose I was told under no circumstances must I open the door in front of me. But then I hear a voice from behind the door say, "Help! Let me out, I'm trapped!" So I open the door when no one is looking. And out comes a huge dog which sinks its teeth into my leg and won't let go. The voice now turns mean. "That was stupid! What were you thinking, you failure?"

The problem is, this dog is invisible. All I know is I did something wrong and now I'm in pain and feel terrible. Who do I get angry with—the dog? No, because I do not know it's there. I get angry with myself.

I confess: "Father God, I opened the door. Please forgive me!" Does He? Of course. In fact, I'm already forgiven.

But I'm still walking around, limping, with an invisible dog hanging off my leg telling me I'm a failure! And that will short-circuit God's power to enable me to live righteously. It makes it difficult for me to resist further temptation or make the right choice.

And the more I seem unable to get out of the cycle, the more the enemy accuses me and the more shame I feel for what I've done.

If we open the door, we allow sin to reign, to become our master. Just confessing sin is not enough. James 4:7 gives us two things to do: submit *and* resist.

Confession is part of submitting. But we must also actively resist the devil and thus reclaim the place of influence that our sin gave him.

Back to our analogy: I start by confessing, "Father God, I opened the door. Please forgive me." Then I tell the dog to let go of my leg and be gone. But why would the dog obey me? Because of who I am now. All of us are identified with Christ, not only in His death and His resurrection, but also in His ascension to the right hand of the Father, where we are seated with Him right now far above all other powers including Satan (Ephesians 2:6).

*For sin will have no dominion over you, since you are
not under law but under grace. (Romans 6:14)*

> SUMMARY

For sin will have no dominion over you, since you are not under law but under
grace. (Romans 6:14)

If we have allowed sin to reign, we can resolve it:

1. Submit to God *and* resist the devil;
2. Know that you are now dead to sin and alive to God;
3. Make the choice every day not to let sin reign in your body by offering every part of
   your body to God rather than to sin.

In any area of your life you are either free or you are a slave. You don't *grow* into freedom. You *take hold* of it.

1. In what ways does the worldview you grew up with either minimize or exaggerate the reality and power of "the spiritual forces of evil in the heavenly places" (Ephesians 6:12)?

2. "In any area of your life you are either free or you are a slave. You don't grow into freedom. You take hold of it." How might this principle change the way you approach getting out of patterns of persistent sin?

> TAKE THE WAY OUT OF TEMPTATION

So how can we resist temptation? The first thing, then, is to ensure we've closed all the doors we opened to the enemy.

> No temptation has overtaken you except what is common to mankind. And God is faithful; he will not let you be tempted beyond what you can bear. But when you are tempted, he will also provide a way out so that you can endure it. (1 Corinthians 10:13 NIV)

The way out that God provides is always right at the beginning of the process of being tempted.

We have to learn to recognize apparently innocent thoughts for what they are—temptation—and "take captive every thought to make it obedient to Christ" (2 Corinthians 10:5 NIV).

Every temptation is an attempt to persuade you to live your life independently of God. Satan knows your history and exactly where you're vulnerable, and that's where he will attack. His aim is to persuade you to try to meet your entirely legitimate needs for acceptance, significance, and security using something other than God.

But God has promised to "meet all your needs according to the riches of his glory in Christ Jesus" (Philippians 4:19 NIV), and we need to learn to find satisfaction only in Him.

Every temptation is based on a lie.

> DRAW NEAR TO THE THRONE OF GRACE

> For we do not have a high priest who is unable to sympathize with our weaknesses, but one who in every respect has been tempted as we are, yet without sin. Let us then with confidence draw near to the throne of grace, that we may receive mercy and find grace to help in time of need. (Hebrews 4:15–16)

Jesus knows what it's like to live in this fallen world with temptation on every side. He knows our weaknesses, and He does not condemn us for them. He actually sympathizes with us.

He invites us to draw near with confidence, not crawl in like miserable worms. If we've gone wrong, we'll find nothing but mercy, forgiveness, and understanding. If we're facing temptation, we'll find grace to overcome.

God loves you so much. No matter where you are right now, He has things for you to do and fruit for you to bear.

What you *do* comes from who you *are*. And you are a pure, holy child of the living God. You are victorious. In fact, you are *more* than a conqueror in Christ!

Draw near. Receive mercy. Find grace to help in your time of need.

REFLECT

Ask the Holy Spirit to speak to you about the two or three temptations that you are most vulnerable to. Write them down. Ask Him why you are particularly vulnerable to these things—is it because of past experiences, for example?

For each one, ask God to identify the lie your vulnerability to sin is based on. Can you think of Bible verses you could use to counteract the lies?

BREAKING SIN-CONFESS CYCLES

Are you frustrated by returning again and again to the same sins?

We invite you to speak out loud the following declaration (based on Romans 6 and James 4).

Instead of depending on your own strength and making rules for yourself to try to keep from sinning, you can enjoy living in the reality of your new identity, Christ in you the hope of glory (Colossians 1:27). Speak it out every day as long as it takes.

> I declare that I am now a new creation in Christ. I am dead to sin and alive to God. I confess my sins [specifically name any habitual sins] and turn away from them.
>
> I specifically declare that the sin of [specifically name any habitual sins one by one] does not rule me any longer, and I renounce its control of me. Jesus, who lives in me, is my loving Master and Ruler, and all that I am now belongs to Him.
>
> Thank You, Jesus, that You have made me a saint, a holy one, so I CAN glorify You in my body. Therefore, I refuse to offer my body to be used to commit unrighteousness. Instead, I submit all that I am to my Heavenly Father, who raised me to life with Christ. I now gladly offer the parts of my body: my heart, eyes, ears, mouth, tongue, hands, feet, sexual organs, mind, understanding, mental powers, emotions, imagination, and reasoning to God, and I choose to use these parts of my body only for righteousness, completely relying on the power of His Holy Spirit within me to accomplish this.
>
> So I submit myself completely to God and resist the devil, who must flee from me now (James 4:7).

WHAT IS "THE STEPS TO EXPERIENCING GOD'S GRACE?"

The Steps To Experiencing God's Grace is a practical session that will help you ensure that the biblical principles we've looked at in *The Grace Course* become real in your experience.

You will ask the Holy Spirit to help you see areas of sin that are giving the enemy some influence in your life. As you submit to God by acknowledging the issues and turning away from them, you will close the "doors" you opened. At the end of the process you will resist the devil, and he will have no option but to flee from you.

All of this is done in a kind and gentle way, and it's just between you and God.

During the process you will be able to identify areas where your beliefs have been out of line with what is actually true according to God's Word, the Bible.

The *Stronghold-Busting* session that directly follows it will equip you with a simple method to demolish those strongholds, one that you can use for the rest of your life whenever you become aware that your belief system is out of kilter with the Bible.

session **05**

COURAGEOUS!

OBJECTIVE

To understand how to deal with unhealthy fears so that they do not control us.

FOCUS VERSE

There is no fear in love, but perfect love casts out fear. For fear has to do with punishment, and whoever fears has not been perfected in love.

1 John 4:18

 ## FOCUS TRUTH

We do not have to allow unhealthy fears to control us or set the agenda in our lives because God is all-powerful and everywhere-present and has given us grace gifts of power, love, and sound judgment.

 ## CONNECT

What were some of the things you were afraid of when growing up?

Read Isaiah 41:10 out loud together:

> So do not fear, for I am with you;
> do not be dismayed, for I am
> your God.
>
> I will strengthen you and help
> you; I will uphold you with my
> righteous right hand. (NIV)

Thank God for these truths.

If you watched *The Wonder Of Grace* introductory video for this session, what was the main thing that struck you?

Was there anything in the YouVersion "Daily Nuggets Of Grace" that especially made you think?

Dear Heavenly Father, thank You that You have promised that You will not leave me or forsake me, and You tell me to be strong and courageous (Joshua 1:5–6). Thank You that Your grace and love are far stronger than any of my fears, so I can confidently say, "You are my helper; I will not fear" (see Hebrews 13:5–6). I will continually praise You and worship You so that I dwell in the truth that You, the all-knowing, everywhere-present, all-powerful, and absolutely loving God of grace, are with me and in me! Amen.

I DECLARE THE TRUTH THAT GOD HAS NOT GIVEN ME A SPIRIT OF FEAR, BUT OF POWER AND LOVE AND A SOUND MIND (2 TIMOTHY 1:7). JESUS IS MY LORD, AND I TELL EVERY ENEMY OF CHRIST TO LEAVE ME NOW. THE SPIRIT I RECEIVED DOES NOT MAKE ME A SLAVE SO THAT I LIVE IN FEAR AGAIN; RATHER, THE SPIRIT I RECEIVED BROUGHT ABOUT MY ADOPTION TO SONSHIP. AND BY HIM I CRY, "ABBA, FATHER" (ROMANS 8:15). GOD IS ON MY SIDE AND WILL DELIVER ME FROM ALL MY FEARS. I AM A BELOVED CHILD OF GOD AND THERE IS NOW NO CONDEMNATION FOR ME BECAUSE I AM IN CHRIST JESUS (ROMANS 8:1).

WORD

COURAGE IS NOT THE ABSENCE OF FEAR

"For we are God's handiwork, created in Christ Jesus to do good works, which God prepared in advance for us to do." (Ephesians 2:10 NIV)

Because of who you now are, God has prepared some specific things for you to do. He doesn't **need** your help, of course, but in His grace He invites you to work with Him.

Maybe that thought fills you with excitement. But it can also be quite scary.

After decades of wandering around the wilderness, the Israelites were to cross the River Jordan and take the land that had been promised to them. And God wanted Joshua to lead them.

That would have been fine if the land was empty. But it wasn't. It was full of people who were exceptionally large and scary. They had a nasty array of weapons, and they were definitely not going to welcome him with open arms!

We get an idea about how Joshua was feeling by what God says to him:

> "Just as I was with Moses, so I will be with you. I will not leave you or forsake you. Be strong and courageous." (Joshua 1:5–6)

God then repeats Himself twice: "Only be strong and very courageous" (v. 7) and "Be strong and courageous" (v. 9) because Joshua was clearly feeling quite the opposite—weak and frightened.

And He adds an instruction, "being careful to do according to all the law that Moses my servant commanded you . . . that you may have good success wherever you go" (v. 7).

There was just one thing Joshua was told to do: to carefully follow God's instructions, God's law. If he did that, God promised him success in this crazy venture to take the land with a rag-tag bunch of wilderness wanderers.

Courage is not the absence of fear. It's making the right choice in the face of that fear.

Fear is another false motivator. Counterintuitively, it's grace that enables us to walk free of it.

> WHAT IS FEAR?

Fear is an emotional reaction to a perception of impending danger or harm that triggers a physical response in our bodies.

When we're confronted by a dangerous situation, our brain quickly evaluates whether it's better to stay and fight, to run away, to keep very still, or to appease the threat. It then sends a signal to our adrenal glands, which pump hormones through our bodies so that we can react rapidly.

Healthy fear is fear that makes sense. For example, it keeps you from petting a snarling, frothing-at-the-mouth dog.

But then there's also **unhealthy fear**. That's fear that is an unreasonable or disproportionate response to what is happening. For example, being afraid of *all* spiders, even the tiny ones that can't harm you at all.

An unhealthy fear works like a boa constrictor. It coils itself around the victim. Each time the victim breathes out, the coils tighten and tighten until the victim is unable to breathe at all.

Unhealthy fears gradually squeeze the joy out of living, making our world smaller and smaller.

More severe fears are known as **phobias;** sometimes they can become so suffocating that people experience "agoraphobia" (literally "fear of the marketplace") and don't want to go out at all.

We may not all have phobias, but most of us are vulnerable to unhealthy fears that can limit what we do if we don't address them.

Fear immobilizes us. It confuses us. It makes it difficult to think straight.

We lose perspective and fear overwhelms us. All you can think about is yourself—your own safety, your own protection, or your own reputation.

> LOVE CASTS OUT FEAR

There is no fear in love; but perfect love casts out fear.

(1 John 4:18)

When fear grips us, we need to come back to the truth of God's Word.

> He has said, "I will never leave you nor forsake you." So we can confidently say, "The Lord is my helper; I will not fear." (Hebrews 13:5–6)

> There is no fear in love; but perfect love casts out fear. (1 John 4:18)

God's love is far stronger than any of our fears. No matter how it *feels*, that is the truth. We can either live in God's grace, or live in fear.

PAUSE FOR THOUGHT 1

1. **What unhealthy fears have you seen at work in your life or in the lives of others? How do you know that they were unhealthy rather than legitimate fears?**

2. **"There is no fear in love; but perfect love casts out fear" (1 John 4:18). How do you think this might work in practice?**

> OVERCOMING UNHEALTHY FEARS

> For God has not given us a spirit of fear, but one of power, love, and sound judgment. (2 Timothy 1:7 CSB)

This verse tells us about three specific grace gifts that enable us to deal a death blow to unhealthy fears.

Note that the verse is written in the past tense. We already have these things. We just need to learn how to use them.

> POWER

Paul prayed this for the Ephesians: "I pray that the eyes of your heart may be enlightened in order that you may know the hope to which he has called you, the riches of his glorious inheritance in his holy people, and his incomparably great *power* for us who believe" (Ephesians 1:18–19 NIV, emphasis added).

Paul doesn't pray that they will *receive* that power, but that they will *know* the power they already have. He goes on to say, "That power is the same as the mighty strength he exerted when he raised Christ from the dead and seated him at his right hand in the heavenly realms, far above all rule and authority, power and dominion, and every name that is invoked, not only in the present age but also in the one to come" (Ephesians 1:19–21 NIV).

He is clearly talking about spiritual power because he mentions Christ's position in the heavenly realms far above all other powers and authorities, meaning demonic powers.

It's the same power that raised Christ from the dead, and you already have it—simply because you are in Christ.

When the enemy plants fearful thoughts in your mind, you can use the power God has given you by saying something like, "Jesus is my Lord and I tell every enemy of Christ to leave now." Or you can declare a truth from God's Word.

> LOVE

> There is no fear in love; but perfect love casts out fear, because fear involves punishment, and the one who fears is not perfected in love. (1 John 4:18 LSB)

If you still believe that God is going to punish you, or is disappointed with you, or that He will stop loving you, then it's impossible to trust Him fully. As a result, you're thrown back onto your own efforts to try to deal with your fears.

But if you remember who you are, a beloved child of God, and that "there is therefore now no condemnation for those who are in Christ Jesus" (Romans 8:1), the fear of His punishment is destroyed.

> SOUND JUDGMENT

"Sound judgment" is sometimes translated as "a sound mind."

Fear distorts the truth. Every unhealthy fear is based on a lie. So exercising sound judgment simply boils down—again!—to coming back to God's Word and making a choice to see things the way God sees them. In other words, how they really are.

God told Joshua not to turn from His Law to the right or the left, so that he would have success wherever he went. It's the same for us.

Making your life count as a disciple of Jesus comes from relentlessly choosing to live according to what God, in His love, tells you in His Word, and to trust God more than you trust the scary thoughts in your mind.

How can we apply sound judgment to unhealthy fears?

For us to have a legitimate healthy fear of something, the thing that we're afraid of must have two qualities. It must be 1) present *and* 2) powerful.

Every unhealthy fear comes from believing that the thing we're afraid of is both present *and* powerful when in fact it isn't.

> THE FEAR OF DEATH

Let's apply sound judgment to the fear of death.

Unless Jesus comes back first, every one of us is going to experience physical death—so we cannot remove the *presence* of death. But what about its *power*?

Hebrews 2:14–15 says that Christ died, "that through death He might render *powerless* him who had the power of death, that is, the devil, and might free those who through fear of death were subject to slavery all their lives" (LSB emphasis added).

And Paul says that death has lost its sting (1 Corinthians 15:55).

But even though the devil is powerless, he can *deceive* us into continuing to live in the fear of death and being slaves to that fear all our lives by making us believe that death is still powerful.

In order for us to be free from slavery to the fear of death, we need to *know* the truth that sets us free: "For to me to live is Christ, and to die is gain" (Philippians 1:21).

If you belong to Jesus, when you die physically, it just gets better. Physical death actually opens the door for you to be with Him in a very tangible way, and to experience all the joys of heaven. Death has no power over us whatsoever!

PAUSE FOR THOUGHT 2

1. **"Behind every unhealthy fear is a lie." Look at the fears below. If someone is prone to those fears, what lies might they believe? For example, a possible lie for the first item on the list is "Satan is more powerful than I am."**

   - **Fear of Satan and powers of darkness**

   - **Fear of the future**

   - **Fear of rejection**

   - **Fear of failure**

   - **Fear of confrontation**

   - **Fear of financial problems**

2. **What truths from God's Word can you find for each lie? For example, for the first item on the list, a good verse would be James 4:7: "Submit . . . to God. Resist the devil, and he will flee from you."**

> THE FEAR OF PEOPLE

The fear of man lays a snare, but whoever trusts in the LORD is safe.
(Proverbs 29:25)

Let's apply sound judgment to the fear of other people.

Above it all, God was in charge. The danger from His enemies was present, but in light of the Creator of the universe, it wasn't powerful.

> AN EXAMPLE

Let's say you have a huge fear of your boss. He's an intimidating person, but right now you are not afraid of him, are you? Why not? He's not here. But when you go to work on Monday morning, there he is.

When you are at the coffee machine having a cup of coffee with your colleagues, you are not afraid of him then, are you? No, because he's over on the other side of the building in his office. Powerful but not present. In fact, you may well want to get off your chest what you think about his character. You are well into your story and completely oblivious. But eventually you turn around and see him—standing there, hands on hips, with a tight smile on his face. Now the fear is healthy! Powerful *and* present.

Or is it? We're told not to fear people (Matthew 10:28). So what can you do to stop the boss from exercising that kind of fear over you even when he's present? You have to get rid of one of those attributes. He's a big guy, so you can't do anything about the fact that he's present. But what about powerful?

Well, exactly what power does he have over you in the worst-case scenario? "He might be able to fire me." True. How can you deal with that? Resign! Well, you don't have to write the letter—but be willing to.

By exercising the sound judgment that God has already given you, by resolving in your own mind today that, if push comes to shove, you will always obey God rather than people and take His opinion of you rather than theirs, you have in effect removed their power. They may be present, but they are no longer powerful.

We need to come to the point where we resolve that our allegiance to King Jesus comes before anything else. Even if those closest to us disapprove of what we're doing for Him, as long as we know that it's the right thing, we will not be afraid of them or their disapproval or rejection but will choose to do the right thing.

In Psalm 56, David gives us the bottom line. "What can man do to me?" he asks (v. 11). And then he answers his own question: "Nothing." He didn't write this in the comfort of his palace but while he was in the hands of his enemies! He had resolved that he could face the worst-case scenario if he was walking in obedience. Above it all, God was in charge. The danger from his enemies was *present*, but in light of the Creator of the universe, it wasn't *powerful*.

> LIVING IN FREEDOM FROM FEAR

How do you live in freedom from fear?

1. DEAL WITH SIN ISSUES

Fear first appeared right after Adam and Eve rebelled. God asked them, "Where are you?" and Adam's response was, "I heard you in the garden, and I was afraid because I was naked; so I hid" (Genesis 3:9–10 NIV).

Sin caused them to feel fear for the first time. And unresolved sin leaves us vulnerable to fear today too. Because it gives the enemy a position of influence in our lives.

2. RECOGNIZE THAT GOD IS ALWAYS PRESENT *AND* ALL POWERFUL

> For those who are led by the Spirit of God are the children of God. The Spirit you received does not make you slaves, so that you live in fear again; rather, the Spirit you received brought about your adoption to sonship. And by him we cry, "Abba, Father." (Romans 8:14–15 NIV)

There is just one fear that is always healthy: the fear of God. Because God is always present and all powerful.

Fear of the Lord does not mean being afraid of Him. It is more like profound awe, a realization of our smallness next to His infinite greatness, a willing submission to our loving Lord and King.

God *is* love. He is on our side. David worked out how to make that truth real. He said, "I sought the LORD, and he answered me; he delivered me from all my fears" (Psalm 34:4 NIV).

"Fear not" is only learned in relationship. Cultivate a lifestyle of praise and worship so that you dwell in the truth that the all-knowing, everywhere-present, all-powerful, and absolutely loving God of grace is with you and in you.

What can a person or anything else do to you? Absolutely nothing!

3. RENEW YOUR MIND

As we've seen, behind every unhealthy fear is a lie. In order to root out the fear, we need to identify the lie and replace it with the truth from God's Word. That's what will transform you.

Before the end of *The Grace Course*, we'll introduce you to Stronghold-Busting, a practical strategy to renew your mind. Imagine how different life would be if you were free from those fears—it's entirely possible!

REFLECT

Read Psalm 145 slowly. Let the words sink in, perhaps by reading it in different versions. Thank God for who He is and what He does. Remind yourself that God never changes and that He is the one who loves you, who is always with you, and who will never leave you nor forsake you.

FREEDOM
IN CHRIST

session **06**

CALM!

OBJECTIVE

To equip us with practical biblical principles that will enable us to cast our anxiety onto Christ and live a life free from inappropriate concern.

FOCUS VERSE

Cast all your anxiety on him because he cares for you.

1 Peter 5:7 NIV

 FOCUS TRUTH

Knowing the character of your Heavenly Father enables you to cast all your anxiety on Him.

 CONNECT

Share a recent picture from your phone or memory that makes you smile.

"I keep my eyes always on the LORD. With him at my right hand, I will not be shaken" (Psalm 16:8 NIV). In times of uncertainty, what character quality of God brings you hope?

If you watched *The Wonder Of Grace* introductory video for this session, what was the main thing that struck you?

Was there anything in the YouVersion "Daily Nuggets Of Grace" that especially made you think?

WORD

WHAT IS ANXIETY?

Fear has a definite object—we are frightened of something *specific*—but anxiety does not. It arises from general uncertainty about the future.

We define anxiety as "a disturbing unease or apprehension that comes from inappropriate concern about something uncertain."

Note that it comes from *inappropriate* concern. It's normal and appropriate to be nervous about an exam you're about to sit or a plane you're about to catch. That anxiety arises from a particular situation but it fades away when it's over. That's not what we're talking about in this session. We will focus on habitual, ongoing anxiety.

Jesus said bluntly, "Do not be anxious about tomorrow" (Matthew 6:34) and Paul says equally plainly, "Do not be anxious about anything" (Philippians 4:6). They would not ask us to do something we could not do.

Perhaps that sounds too simplistic. After all, anxiety can have complex causes such as stress or past trauma. But bear with us as we look at how living in God's grace can prevent us from being at the mercy of every anxious thought, no matter what circumstances we find ourselves in.

> HUMBLE YOURSELF

Humble yourselves, therefore, under God's mighty hand, that he may lift you up in due time. Cast all your anxiety on him because he cares for you. (1 Peter 5:6–7 NIV)

Does God have a mighty hand? Yes! He is all-powerful.

Does He care for you? Yes! He *is* love. He has good plans for you. He *will* lift you up in due time.

Humbling yourself before God is essentially no more than making a choice to believe that these things are true and then acting accordingly.

> ADOPT GOD'S GOAL FOR YOUR LIFE

Part of humbling yourself before God is making the choice to bring your major life-goals into line with His goal for you.

What are you hoping to achieve some day? Career success? Getting married and having children? Seeing your children achieve certain things? Having a successful Christian ministry?

Those can be good things. But you can never be sure that they are going to happen—a successful outcome depends on other people or circumstances that are not under your direct control. So if you measure your personal worth or success by whether or not they are achieved, you will experience anxiety.

God's goal for all of us is not so much about what we *do* or *achieve* but what we're *like*.

It's about our character: becoming more loving, kind, patient, etc.

God's goal for us is to become more and more like Jesus in character.

What or who can stop that from happening? Nothing and no one! So there's no uncertainty and therefore no anxiety.

What if a difficult person attacks me unfairly or gets in my way? Or what if I get a really bad health issue? Or my business fails? None of those things can stop you from becoming more and more like Jesus. In fact, if you rely on God and persevere through those difficulties, they will actually *help* you become more and more like Jesus.

> GET OFF THE FENCE

James describes someone who, in the face of uncertainty and anxiety-causing circumstances, asks God for wisdom but then, instead of persevering through the difficult situations, doubts God and falls back on their own resources. He says, "Such a person is double-minded and unstable in all they do" (James 1:8 NIV).

The Greek word for *anxiety* in the New Testament is a combination of two words meaning "divide" and "mind." Anxiety literally meant being in two minds (double-minded)—constantly going back and forth.

Unless you have made that definite choice to trust God and follow His ways come what may, you will always be in two minds and, therefore, unstable and anxious.

PAUSE FOR THOUGHT 1

1. Share an occasion when anxiety has caused you to be "double-minded" and led to instability in your walk with God.

2. What do you think it looks like in practice to "humble yourself under the mighty hand of God" when you face anxiety?

> RESOLVING ANXIETY

Satan is actively trying to get us into anxiety and to exploit the double-mindedness it causes.

> Humble yourselves, therefore, under God's mighty hand, that he may lift you up in due time. Cast all your anxiety on him because he cares for you. (1 Peter 5:6–7 NIV)

> Be alert and of sober mind. Your enemy the devil prowls around like a roaring lion looking for someone to devour. Resist him, standing firm in the faith, because you know that the family of believers throughout the world is undergoing the same kind of sufferings. (1 Peter 5:8–9 NIV)

You probably know both of these passages well. But did you realize that they are actually one passage with the second directly following the first? In other words, they are part of the same argument.

Our struggle with anxiety is not just between us and circumstances. Satan is actively trying to get us into anxiety and to exploit the double-mindedness it causes.

At the end of this course, you will go through *The Steps To Experiencing God's Grace*, a practical session that recognizes the reality of the spiritual battle we are in and will help you deal with the things that are preventing you from experiencing and living in God's grace in that context.

The sixth Step in the process is called "Exchanging Anxiety For God's Peace," and the biblical principles behind it are outlined below. Once you know them, you can use them whenever you realize that anxiety has begun to take hold.

1. PRAY

> Be anxious for nothing, but in everything by prayer and petition with thanksgiving let your requests be made known to God. (Philippians 4:6 LSB)

Prayer focuses your mind on God, His character, and His love. It takes our focus off our anxiety and puts our attention on the One who cares for us.

And when you pray, don't forget to give thanks. Thanksgiving focuses your attention on what God has done in the past, and what He is already doing in your current situation.

2. STATE THE PROBLEM

When we're anxious, we struggle to put things into perspective. The process of worrying usually takes a greater toll on us than the worst-case scenario in our thoughts.

A problem well-stated is half-solved. Clarifying the issue and putting it into perspective can bring tremendous relief.

Will this particular thing that you feel uncertain about matter for eternity?

3. FOCUS ON FACTS AND REJECT ASSUMPTIONS

We are anxious because we do not know what is going to happen. And because we do not know, we tend to make assumptions.

For many of us, our minds leap to the worst possible outcome, and, before we know it, we've convinced ourselves that is what's going to happen! In the vast majority of cases, of course, the worst doesn't happen. So stick to the facts of the situation.

4. DETERMINE YOUR RESPONSIBILITIES

Work out prayerfully before God in the situation that is causing your anxiety:

- What is *your* responsibility?
- What is *God's* responsibility?
- and what is *someone else's* responsibility?

The key principle is that you can be responsible only for the things that you have both the *right* and *ability* to control. You are not responsible for things where that is not the case. Generally speaking, the things God has given you the right and ability to control will boil down to things in your own life. And if you are not living a responsible life, then you probably should feel anxious!

Once you have clarified what you are responsible for, then fulfill your responsibilities. Don't just pray about them. You can cast your anxieties onto Jesus, but if you try casting your responsibilities onto Him, He will throw them right back to you!

Once you have fulfilled your responsibility, you can confidently cast your anxiety onto Him, saying, "Now it's up to You, God."

You can be sure that He will play His part. So leave it with Him. Don't pick it up again.

> PRACTICAL HELPS

There are some simple, practical things we can all do to help our bodies calm down so that we can better focus on God, which will naturally then reduce our anxiety.

- Get outdoors and drink in the beauty of God's creation.
- Take regular physical exercise if you can.
- Control your use of phones, tablets, and other gadgets—constantly flicking from one thing to another gives us the illusion of multi-tasking or de-stressing, but it actually destroys our ability to concentrate and makes us feel anxious.

See "Physical Tips To Combat Anxiety" on page 79.

> DWELLING IN APPRECIATION

Whatever is true, whatever is honorable, whatever is just, whatever is pure, whatever is lovely, whatever is commendable, if there is any excellence, if there is anything worthy of praise, think about these things. What you have learned and received and heard and seen in me—practice these things, and the God of peace will be with you. (Philippians 4:8–9)

Paul is telling us to make a conscious choice about what we focus on. This is not "the power of positive thinking"—it is much better than that. We focus on truth. We "marinate" in thanksgiving, letting our hearts become tender.

Praise and worship remind us that God is present, that He is real, and that He is for us. That can calm us like nothing else!

When we practice dwelling on what is true and lovely and just and worthy of praise, we have God's wonderful promise—the God of peace *will* be with you!

See "Dwelling In Appreciation" on page 80.

PAUSE FOR THOUGHT 2

1. **How have you seen prayer with thanksgiving combat anxiety?**

2. **What practical measures from this section would you like to implement? Share any other practical tips you have learned to overcome anxiety.**

> SEEING GOD AS HE IS

If you want the truth to set you free, you have to know *the truth.*

The reason you *can* cast your anxiety onto God is because He cares for you. He is the God of grace. He *is* real, He *is* strong, and He *is* love.

But, as we've seen, if you're not sure He genuinely cares for you, you may bring a concern to Him and ask for His help, but then you will pick it back up and try to solve it yourself.

If you want the truth to set you free, you have to *know* the truth. Jesus said, "I *am* the Truth" (John 14:6). Truth is not just a concept but a person. And you have to know that person.

What makes this tricky is that the world and the devil feed us caricatures of God and lies about Him that keep us from really knowing Him.

Our experiences with our parents and other authority figures also shape our view of our Heavenly Father. So we need to unravel some distorted images if we are to know God as He really is.

Perhaps your experiences have led you to believe that God is unjust. Or that He's unkind or even cruel. Maybe you feel God is hard to please.

Read (out loud if possible) the powerful statements about "My Father God" on pages 81–82.

Is there a place where the words seem to stick in your throat? Bring those to Jesus.

If you realize you have a faulty understanding of God, reading this list out loud every day for six weeks or so can help dramatically.

REFLECT

Which truth about your Father God is most meaningful to you? How has your view of God been conditioned by experiences of your own father? Ask God to show you where He was in those times when He seemed less than kind and compassionate, or when He seemed absent or uninvolved, and wait for His response. Thank Him for who He is and for being a perfect Father to you.

PHYSICAL TIPS TO COMBAT ANXIETY

The major way to combat anxiety is through the biblical principles outlined in this session, but there are some other things that can help too. God has made our physical bodies to an incredible design that includes some inbuilt ways to counter anxiety. You may sometimes find yourself subconsciously massaging your arms or rubbing your face—these are small practices that are helping calm your body down.

Here are some other practices you can do:

Belly breathing—slow and low. This helps deactivate the fight or flight response.

- Inhale to the count of four, letting your diaphragm expand, hold to the count of four, exhale to the count of four and say a Bible verse, perhaps Psalm 56:3, "When I am afraid, I will trust in You" (LSB). Then pause and count to four. Repeat three times.

- You could say a name of God like "Lord Jesus" as you inhale, and a Bible verse prayer as you exhale, e.g., "Help me to be still and know that you are God" (see Psalm 46:10).

- Or you could make a simple affirmation, e.g., "I breathe in your peace. I breathe out your praise."

Take part in worship as the Bible continually exhorts us to: "Let us sing, let us shout to the God of our salvation, let us worship and bow down, let us exalt His name together, let us raise our hearts and hands toward God in heaven" (see Psalm 95). Dr. Richard Smith, head of the Mercy Hospital Neuroscience Institute, found that participatory worship brings about a decrease in blood pressure, a slower pulse, and a reduction in anger and depression.[1]

Tense and then release various muscle groups from your head to your toes. This is something you can do discreetly if a difficult situation arises.

Try yawning. Yawning signals to your body that it is time to quiet and rest. Turn your head to the left, yawn—and then the opposite way and yawn. The result is that more oxygen flows to the brain. One article called it the "fastest way to hack mental stress and focus."[2]

Laugh and play. "A joyful heart is good medicine" (Proverbs 17:22). In Proverbs 8:31, we find God rejoicing in His creation and taking delight in the human beings He created. *John Gill's Exposition of the Bible* says that the word chosen indicates that "it was a kind of sport or play unto him." In other words, it is not just okay to play, but God is actually the author of play.

Physical exercise works wonders. Strenuous exercise releases endorphins, which relieve pain and create a sense of well-being. Walking at a little slower pace gives us time to drink in God's beauty in creation.

---

1. From his talk "Praise, Worship, Thanksgiving, and Brain Neurotransmitters."
2. Josiah Hultgren, "Yawning is The Fastest Way to Hack Mental Stress and Focus," June 20, 2016, Medium.com, retrieved November 20, 2023, https://medium.com/mindfullyalive/yawning-is-the-fastest-way-to-hack-mental-stress-and-focus-f693edc9f55e.

DWELLING IN APPRECIATION

When we practice dwelling in appreciation of God, His character, His love, and His works, it changes us. We'll know the true awe and wonder of God—what the Bible calls "fearing the Lord"—and won't be in fear of anything or anyone at all! (See Psalm 130:4.)

It's not so much about making a list of things you're thankful for but taking time with Him and, as Paul describes in Philippians 4:8–9, **dwelling on** "whatever is true, whatever is honorable, whatever is just, whatever is pure, whatever is lovely, whatever is commendable, if there is any excellence, if there is anything worthy of praise."

Here is an approach we recommend that will help you develop a lifestyle of praise and worship that springs from appreciation. You may well find it life-changing!

DRAW NEAR

- "Enter his gates with thanksgiving, and his courts with praise!" (Psalm 100:4). **Draw near** to His presence through thanksgiving and praise.

DWELL

- **Dwell** on these things. Marinate in thanksgiving. Describe in detail to God what you noticed, liked, and appreciated about Him or His works. How did you feel physically as you appreciated Him? Let your heart become tender.

PRACTICE

- **Practice** dwelling—because practice is definitely required! And we have God's wonderful promise: the God of peace will be with you! So do this on a regular basis. It can be very helpful to **build an appreciation file** full of appreciation memories with God. Files help you to bring things to mind readily. These memories will help you make the choice to trust in God, who is the Truth, when circumstances tell you to doubt Him.

LISTEN FOR HIS VOICE

- The practice of appreciating God allows us to hear the voice of God. Psalm 95 begins by saying, "O come, let us sing for joy to the LORD, let us shout joyfully to the rock of our salvation. Let us come before His presence with thanksgiving, let us shout joyfully to Him with psalms." Then it goes on to say, "Today, if you would hear His voice, do not harden your hearts" (vv. 7–8 NASB 1995). Dwelling in appreciation prepares the way to hear God's voice, so **listen for His voice**.

MY FATHER GOD

I reject the lie that You, Father God, are distant and uninterested in me.

I choose to believe the truth that You, Father God, are always personally present with me, have plans to give me a hope and a future, and have prepared works in advance specifically for me to do.

(Psalm 139:1–18; Matthew 28:20; Jeremiah 29:11; Ephesians 2:10)

I reject the lie that You, Father God, are insensitive and don't know me or care for me.

I choose to believe the truth that You, Father God, are kind and compassionate and know every single thing about me.

(Psalm 103:8–14; 1 John 3:1–3; Hebrews 4:12–13)

I reject the lie that You, Father God, are stern and have placed unrealistic expectations on me.

I choose to believe the truth that You, Father God, have accepted me and are joyfully supportive of me.

(Romans 15:7; Zephaniah 3:17)

I reject the lie that You, Father God, are passive and cold toward me.

I choose to believe the truth that You, Father God, are warm and affectionate toward me.

(Isaiah 40:11; Hosea 11:3–4)

I reject the lie that You, Father God, are absent or too busy for me.

I choose to believe the truth that You, Father God, are always present and eager to be with me and enable me to be all that You created me to be.

(Philippians 1:6; Hebrews 13:5)

I reject the lie that You, Father God, are impatient or angry with me, or have rejected me.

I choose to believe the truth that You, Father God, are patient and slow to anger, and that when You discipline me, it is a proof of Your love, and not rejection.

(Exodus 34:6; Romans 2:4; Hebrews 12:5–11)

I reject the lie that You, Father God, have been mean, cruel, or abusive to me.

I choose to believe the truth that Satan is mean, cruel, and abusive, but You, Father God, are loving, gentle, and protective.

(Psalm 18:2; Matthew 11:28–30; Ephesians 6:10–18)

I reject the lie that You, Father God, are denying me the pleasures of life.

I choose to believe the truth that You, Father God, are the author of life and will lead me into love, joy, and peace when I choose to be filled with Your Spirit.

(Lamentations 3:22–23; Galatians 5:22–24)

I reject the lie that You, Father God, are trying to control and manipulate me.

I choose to believe the truth that You, Father God, have set me free, and give me the freedom to make choices and grow in Your grace.

(Galatians 5:1; Hebrews 4:15–16)

I reject the lie that You, Father God, have condemned me, and no longer forgive me.

I choose to believe the truth that You, Father God, have forgiven all my sins and will never use them against me in the future.

(Jeremiah 31:31–34; Romans 8:1)

I reject the lie that You, Father God, reject me when I fail to live a perfect or sinless life.

I choose to believe the truth that You, Father God, are patient toward me and cleanse me when I fail.

(Proverbs 24:16; 1 John 1:7–2:2)

I AM THE APPLE OF YOUR EYE!

(Deuteronomy 32:9–10)

session **07**

FRUITFUL!

OBJECTIVE

To help us bear more and more fruit as disciples of Jesus by resting in God, trusting in His ways, and offering our whole selves to Him as living sacrifices.

FOCUS VERSE

"I am the vine; you are the branches. Whoever abides in me and I in him,
he it is that bears much fruit, for apart from me you can do nothing."

John 15:5

 ## FOCUS TRUTH

If we want to be fruitful, our focus needs to be not on bearing fruit but on staying close to Jesus and humbling ourselves to live according to God's ways as revealed in the Bible.

 ## CONNECT

Some people are said to have a "green thumb" because of their success in growing plants. What is your track record in this area?

In John 15, Jesus compares Himself to a vine, and us to branches of that vine. How does it encourage you to know that He also says that Father God is the gardener?

If you watched *The Wonder Of Grace* introductory video for this session, what was the main thing that struck you?

Was there anything in the YouVersion "Daily Nuggets Of Grace" that especially made you think?

WORD

HOW TO BEAR FRUIT

"I am the true vine, and my Father is the gardener. He cuts off every branch in me that bears no fruit, while every branch that does bear fruit he prunes so that it will be even more fruitful. You are already clean because of the word I have spoken to you. Remain in me, as I also remain in you. No branch can bear fruit by itself; it must remain in the vine. Neither can you bear fruit unless you remain in me. I am the vine; you are the branches. If you remain in me and I in you, you will bear much fruit; apart from me you can do nothing." (John 15:1–5 NIV)

What is a branch's one responsibility? We might think it is to bear fruit, but it's more fundamental than that. Jesus says it is to remain in the vine. Then it will automatically bear fruit.

Our responsibility is to "remain" in Jesus, to stay connected to Him, to keep close to Him. This is the key to entering a life of "grace-rest" where, paradoxically, we *will* bear lots of fruit.

"The Son can do nothing by himself; he can do only what he sees his Father doing" (John 5:19 NIV).

Even though He was God, He wasn't operating out of His "God-ness." But He was modeling how *we* are to live. He simply focused on being in a loving relationship with the Father. Then He saw what the Father was doing and joined in.

If you *strain* to bear fruit, to achieve some kind of success—a ministry position or some other target—it doesn't work because you remove yourself from a grace-based trust in Jesus, where you know that you can do nothing apart from Him. Instead, you put yourself into a law-based system of anxious performance, where everything depends on you. And you just can't make it *all* happen.

> PRINCIPLE 1: APART FROM JESUS WE CAN DO *NOTHING*

When we believe that it all comes down to our own efforts, we risk burning out or being overwhelmed.

To help us learn, God will often allow us to struggle under the burden of trying to do it ourselves. If *you* are feeling that pressure, Jesus makes you an offer:

"Come to me, all who labor and are heavy laden, and I will give you rest. Take my yoke upon you, and learn from me, for I am gentle and lowly in heart, and you will find rest for your souls. For my yoke is easy, and my burden is light." (Matthew 11:28–30)

God genuinely offers us a yoke that is easy, a burden that is light, and rest for our soul.

The rest He offers does not mean lying around doing nothing. It is an internal rest. It means that you truly follow His lead and go at His pace.

TRUST GOD, BEAR FRUIT

> *First we rest in God's reality and provision, and then we work. We learn to trust God, then we bear fruit.*

When God made the world He worked for six days and then rested on the seventh. God "rested" in the sense that His all-powerful reign over the universe began and all was as it should be.

Adam was created on day six, so the first full day of his life was that day of rest, a day of *connecting* with God, *knowing* that God was in charge, and *actively trusting* Him.

First we rest in God's reality and provision, and then we work. We learn to trust God, then we bear fruit.

It's not enough to know Jesus as Savior, or even as King. We need to come to realize that He is our very Life (see Colossians 3:4).

Understanding this enables us to leave behind that false motivator of pride that leads to anxious performance. We do not need to try to control events or people. We can trust God to take care of the things that are outside our control. We come to see that He really does work in all things for our good (Romans 8:28).

PAUSE FOR THOUGHT 1

1. Read John 5:19–20. In what ways did Jesus' life on earth demonstrate His complete dependence upon the Father?

2. In what ways might our lives look different if we depended completely on God?

> PRINCIPLE 2: FRUITFULNESS COMES ONLY WHEN WE SUBMIT TO GOD AND DO WHAT HE SAYS

God revealed to Simon Peter, one of Jesus' disciples, that Jesus was the Son of God. Jesus explained to him even more of God's plans, including that He was going to have to suffer and die. But Peter interrupted Him and told Him He was wrong.

Peter has just understood that he's face-to-face with God Himself, and his response is to tell the Creator of the Universe that He has got it all wrong. How arrogant can you get?

Adam's downfall came when Satan persuaded him that he too knew better than God. All of us are prone to pride.

"As the heavens are higher than the earth, so are my ways higher than your ways and my thoughts than your thoughts." (Isaiah 55:9)

"Trust in the LORD with all your heart and lean not on your own understanding; in all your ways submit to him, and he will make your paths straight." (Proverbs 3:5–6 NIV)

Instead of acting out of pride and trusting our own understanding, our worldview, or our past experiences, we need to learn to trust what God says. He promises that, when we do, he will "make our paths straight" and we can expect our lives to be fruitful.

> THE BIBLE REVEALS GOD'S WAYS

God has revealed in the Bible what He is like, how He has set up the world, and our part in His plans.

Satan does not want you to take it seriously, or read it for yourself, or spend time with God each day humbling yourself before Him and His Word. He wants to make us think that we know better than God.

> The Spirit clearly says that in later times some will abandon the faith and follow deceiving spirits and things taught by demons. (1 Timothy 4:1 NIV)

Even people who claim to be Christians will follow the teaching of demons. Do not be surprised if you hear Christian teachers implying that the Bible does not say what it plainly does say.

Satan used the phrase, "Did God *really* say?" (Genesis 3:1). And he uses that line with us too.

HUMBLING OURSELVES BEFORE GOD AND HIS WORD

God promises to guide you into all truth by His Spirit.

God promises to guide you into all truth by His Spirit. If you approach His Word with a humble, teachable spirit, you *will* understand what He has to say to you.

- Do not just listen to others talk about the Bible or just read Bible study notes: read it for yourself.

- Take what it says seriously.

- Do not come to it with a preconceived idea of what you want it to say, even if your intentions seem good. Focus on what it *actually* says.

- Do not filter what is written plainly in the Bible through the theology you have been taught—judge what you have been taught according to what the Bible says.

- If a passage does not make immediate sense, do not skip over it. Persevere, ask, research, and listen until you understand why the God who is love included it.

- Try to understand the culture it was written for, and do not make it say anything that the original hearers could not have understood from it.

God never changes. And truth never changes. Our theology, on the other hand, is our attempt to understand God and His truth. As we grow as Christians, our understanding develops and our theology can change. We will always be learning more about God and His ways as He reveals them to us through His Word.

PAUSE FOR THOUGHT 2

1. **How can we prevent ourselves from being deceived in our understanding of the Bible?**

2. **How might well-meaning people be tempted to twist the Bible to match their own biases and preferences?**

> PRINCIPLE 3: THE GATEWAY TO FRUITFULNESS IS BROKENNESS

"Every branch that *does* bear fruit he prunes so that it will be even more fruitful." (John 15:2 NIV)

Pruning is painful but it is done to those who are already bearing fruit in order that they might bear even more. Even Jesus "learned obedience through what he suffered" (Hebrews 5:8).

God is continually working to cut away our self-centeredness, self-reliance, and pride.

All discipline for the moment seems not to be joyful, but sorrowful; yet to those who have been trained by it, afterwards it yields the peaceful fruit of righteousness. (Hebrews 12:11 NASB 1995)

God isn't the cause of every difficulty. But He will use every difficulty for our good. He never wastes any experience. Tough times are where we learn to trust Him.

When God gave Paul a difficult situation specifically to prevent him from becoming proud, Paul asked Him three times to take it away. But God said, "My grace is sufficient for you, for my power is made perfect in weakness" (2 Corinthians 12:9). We are not saying we should enjoy difficulties. But they are not always things to be "prayed out of the way."

My heart is not proud, LORD, my eyes are not haughty; I do not concern myself with great matters or things too wonderful for me. (Psalm 131:1 NIV)

This is *King* David. He *does* deal with "great matters." He makes life and death decisions every day. But here he simply recognizes that if he thought he could do them in his own strength, it would be pride.

Then he says, "No, right now I am calm and quiet, like a child after nursing, content in its mother's arms." (Psalm 131:2 ERV)

Deep inside us there's a part that cries out restlessly like a hungry infant. It can be from shame, guilt, fear, fleshly urges, or pride.

But, by persevering through extreme difficulties when King Saul was hunting him down, David learned to rest in God. To allow God alone to satisfy him.

BECOME A LIVING SACRIFICE

> I urge you, brothers and sisters, in view of God's mercy, to offer your bodies as a living sacrifice, holy and pleasing to God (Romans 12:1 NIV).

The idea of a live animal being placed on an altar as a *living* sacrifice is amusing—because it can jump up and run away!

But think about the hours that Jesus hung on the cross in incredible agony, every breath a massive, painful effort, until His heart burst from the strain. A literal living sacrifice.

Choosing to make ourselves a living sacrifice is a response to God's mercy:

- Jesus became a sacrifice for you, paying an unimaginable price so that you are now declared completely innocent.

- Jesus became sin on your behalf, and you became the righteousness of God, a holy one.

- You are now safe and secure. No one can take you out of His hands. And His love can drive out every unhealthy fear.

- You can cast all your anxiety on Him and walk in peace, because He cares for you.

- You are genuinely free. Free from the power of sin, the power of Satan, and the power of death. Free to make good choices.

- You need only focus on remaining in Him in order to bear lots of fruit.

- You are now secure enough in who you are in Christ to humble yourself before God and before others. With no need to try to control events or people.

- You know that you can do absolutely nothing in your own strength but that He can do absolutely anything through you.

You are a son or daughter of the King of Kings, dressed in your rich robe, your ring of authority, and your sandals. And God Himself is looking at you with eyes of pure love and delight.

Will you choose to lay down everything at His feet: your health, your plans, your money, your family, your ministry, your future? To make Jesus your King—and your very Life?

It's okay to come like the younger son in complete weakness and just collapse. God will run to you and embrace you. He will never abandon you. He will never take you beyond what you can bear as He gives you strength.

Here are some words you might like to use as you pray:

Loving Father God,

Thank You for sending Jesus, Who, being in very nature God, did not consider equality with God something to be used to His own advantage but made Himself nothing and humbled Himself by becoming obedient to death—even death on a cross.

I choose right now to trust in You with all my heart. I deliberately turn away from relying on my own understanding. I submit to You in all my ways, in every part of my life. Thank You that You will make my paths straight.

Thank You for the Bible, Your clear Word to us. I pray that You will help me understand it in all of its wonderful fullness as I come with an open heart ready to hear Your instructions, encouragement, and correction. I refuse to water Your Word down, gloss it over, or try to make it say what I think it should say. Thank You that your Holy Spirit will lead me into all truth.

Please help me root out the deeply ingrained lies I have believed and replace them with truth so that I may truly be transformed by the renewing of my mind.

As a response to Your grace, I choose here and now to offer you my body and all that I am as a living sacrifice, holy and pleasing to You. This is my true and proper worship.

And I worship You now.

Amen.

God was not the cause of all the difficult things you have experienced in your life, but He does promise to work in them and turn them around to good. In this time, cast your mind back to difficult times in your life and ask God to show you how He was working in them. What fruit can you see in your own character or life from those experiences?

Paul said he could be "content with weaknesses, insults, hardships, persecutions, and calamities" (2 Corinthians 12:10). Do you think he really meant that? Tell God how you feel about the gateway to fruitfulness being brokenness.

session **08**

PEACEMAKER!

OBJECTIVE

To help us understand the crucial role of the Church, the Body and Bride of Christ, in God's plans and why a passionate commitment to maintaining the unity of the Spirit in the bond of peace is vital if we are to reach this world for Christ.

FOCUS VERSE

"By this all people will know that you are my disciples, if you have love for one another."

John 13:35

 ## FOCUS TRUTH

Unity is key to exercising the spiritual authority to disciple the nations that Jesus delegated to us.

 ## CONNECT

If you were writing a book about your life, what would you like the title of the next chapter to be?

Read Psalm 133:

> How good and pleasant it is when God's people live together in unity! It is like precious oil poured on the head, running down on the beard, running down on Aaron's beard, down on the collar of his robe. It is as if the dew of Hermon were falling on Mount Zion. For there the LORD bestows his blessing, even life forevermore. (NIV)

Where have you seen unity bring blessing?

If you watched *The Wonder Of Grace* introductory video for this session, what was the main thing that struck you?

Was there anything in the YouVersion "Daily Nuggets Of Grace" that especially made you think?

WORD

JESUS DELEGATES SPIRITUAL AUTHORITY TO US

Jesus does not simply command us to go and make disciples. He starts by stating a crucial prerequisite: "All authority in heaven and on earth has been given to me." Only on that basis does He then go on to say, *"Therefore*, go and make disciples . . ." (see Matthew 28:16–20).

At the cross Jesus "disarmed the powers and authorities, [and] he made a public spectacle of them" (Colossians 2:15 NIV). He is now seated at the right hand of the Father far above every demonic power and authority.

And He delegates that spiritual authority to us. Why? Specifically in order to disciple the nations.

Why do we need it?

"The god of this age has blinded the minds of unbelievers, so that they cannot see the light of the gospel that displays the glory of Christ, who is the image of God." (2 Corinthians 4:4 NIV)

If Satan is keeping people in spiritual blindness, just telling them the gospel will not always work. They cannot see it. It's a spiritual problem, and we address it with the spiritual authority over Satan that Jesus has delegated to us.

How do we activate this authority?

"By this all people will know that you are my disciples, *if you have love for one another.*" (John 13:35, emphasis added)

And the one thing Jesus chose to pray for us, who come after His original disciples, is that we would all be one, just as He and the Father are one. Why?

"So that the world may believe that you have sent me" (John 17:21).

Psalm 133 tells us that it is in unity that "the LORD has commanded the blessing, life forevermore."

We activate our delegated authority when we love each other.

The early Church had no real resources but was totally united. Thousands of people at a time had their eyes opened to the light of the gospel and responded to it.

Together we are God's chosen instrument to disciple the nations. There is no Plan B.

> THE BODY OF CHRIST

The New Testament continually urges us to be united and talks of us as "the Body of Christ." It's more than just a metaphor: we are the actual flesh and blood, the arms and legs, through whom God works in the world.

As individual Christians on our own, we are like a dismembered leg or a single eye—no use whatsoever without the rest of the body.

Our definition of unity is "a shared passion for God, and for His purposes, that is so strong that it overrides our different preferences and opinions."

Jesus said, "Blessed are the peacemakers, for they will be called children of God" (Matthew 5:9 NIV). If you are a child of God, living out of your identity in Christ, you will be a peacemaker.

> FIND YOUR PLACE IN THE BODY

If you are not already part of a local church fellowship, can we encourage you to join one?

If He has not made you the leader, follow those whom God has chosen to lead. Unless they are clearly overstepping the bounds of their authority or are in obvious sin, it's our job to encourage and support them—warts and all.

Persevere when it gets tough—and it will.

Commit yourself to love and unity. Satan understands the power of our unity and will relentlessly tempt us into disunity. There's a great biblical principle: "If it is possible, as far as it depends on you, live at peace with everyone" (Romans 12:18 NIV). We are to do what is in our power to do and leave the rest to the other person and to God.

Learn to forgive, relentlessly. This is painful and costly but, although you let the person off your hook, they are not off God's hook. You can hand all of that pain, and those demands for justice and revenge, over to God, safe in the knowledge that justice will be done. In the meantime you can walk free of it, and you can prevent Satan from getting a foothold in your church fellowship (see Romans 12:19).

As far as it depends on us, let's do everything we can to unleash the spiritual power that unity brings in the place where God has put us.

PAUSE FOR THOUGHT 1

1. "Together we are God's chosen instrument to disciple the nations. There is no Plan B." Do you find this statement encouraging or daunting? Why?

2. Why, of all the things He could have prayed for those of us who would come after the first disciples, do you think that Jesus chose to pray that we would be one?

> APPROACHING THOSE WHO DO NOT YET KNOW JESUS

You cannot preach the good news but be the bad news.

We saw in Session 3 how the Church in many places came to see itself as responsible for the morals of the whole nation. Instead of astonishing people by our acts of love and showing that we are *for* them, we have become known for what we are *against*.

You cannot preach the good news but be the bad news.

Does God want us to tell people what they're doing wrong?

> I wrote to you in my letter not to associate with sexually immoral people—not at all meaning *the people of this world* who are immoral, or the greedy and swindlers, or idolaters. In that case you would have to leave this world. But now I am writing to you that you must not associate with anyone who claims to be *a brother or sister* but is sexually immoral or greedy, an idolater or slanderer, a drunkard or swindler. (1 Corinthians 5:9–11 NIV)

The Corinthians had assumed that Paul meant they should not associate with sexually immoral people *outside* the church. But Paul says that when it comes

to these sin issues, our concern should rather be those *inside* the Church who persistently sin.

In Romans 1, Paul explains in graphic detail the dire situation that those who do not yet know Jesus are in: their thinking has become futile, their hearts are "darkened" and they indulge in impurity, unnatural sexual passions, murder, deceit, pride, and heartlessness (see Romans 1:18–32). He affirms that "the judgment of God rightly falls on those who practice such things" (Romans 2:2).

He then gives a stern warning:

> Do you suppose, O man—you who judge those who practice such things and yet do them yourself— that you will escape the judgment of God? Or do you presume on the riches of his kindness and forbearance and patience, not knowing that God's kindness is meant to lead you to repentance? (Romans 2:2–4)

This warning is not for the people out in the world who are actually caught in these things. It's for Christians who, despite having experienced God's grace, let their own standards slip—and yet feel free to condemn others.

The kindness of God that they had experienced was meant to lead them to repentance, not give them freedom to sin. It's *kindness* not condemnation that leads people to repentance.

But if we do not point out the sin in the world, doesn't that send a message that what they are doing is okay?

Jesus did not point out the sin of Zaccheus the tax collector, yet he promised to repay everything he had stolen. A prostitute made an extravagant public display of repentance, and Jesus had not said a word.

God does not want us to judge people for their brokenness. He wants us to show them the way out of it.

Every single person should know they are welcome in our churches, no matter what kind of darkness they are living in.

> APPROACHING THOSE WHO DO KNOW JESUS

Once someone turns to Christ, we don't encourage them to continue living in ways that God warns against. We expect to see dramatic change. Jesus wants His Church to reflect the purity and holiness that He has given her.

We do not start by telling new Christians what's wrong with them—we need to start by telling them what's right with them! What we do comes from who we are! They need to know that they are now holy, that they are loved, and that Jesus calls them to incredible fruitfulness.

They also need to know that, when God tells us not to do something, it's not because He's some kind of killjoy. It's because Jesus came specifically to set them free from slavery to sin.

> Out of the same mouth come praise and cursing. My brothers and sisters, this should not be. Can both fresh water and salt water flow from the same spring? My brothers and sisters, can a fig tree bear olives, or a grapevine bear figs? Neither can a salt spring produce fresh water. (James 3:10–12 NIV)

James does not use harsh words to correct a sin issue. He just makes the simple point that a fresh water spring does not produce salt water—it just doesn't. And a fig tree does not bear olives—of course it doesn't. And if I lose my temper, grumble, or dwell on a lustful thought, I am acting out of character.

Deep down inside we are now holy ones. And, if everything is working as it should, we'll do the things that holy ones do. It really is as simple as that.

If people refuse to respond to the gentle approach, on rare occasions church leaders will need to exercise discipline. Out of love. This is not about punishing people. Godly discipline is about helping them not to make the same mistake again. It's about restoration. It's kind.

It is kindness, not condemnation, that leads people to repentance.

PAUSE FOR THOUGHT 2

1. How do you think it works that kindness leads people to repentance? Where have you seen this happening?

2. How can telling new Christians what is right with them (now that they are in Christ) help them become fruitful disciples?

3. How would you sum up the differences in the way we are called to approach those outside the Body of Christ compared to those inside?

Unity enables us to exercise our spiritual authority to make disciples.

> WHAT IS TRUE UNITY?

Paul tells us to be "eager to maintain the unity of the Spirit in the bond of peace" (Ephesians 4:3). No wonder, because that is what enables us to exercise our spiritual authority to make disciples.

That word *maintain* tells us we are already united at one level. But who exactly are we united with?

> If you declare with your mouth, "Jesus is Lord," and believe in your heart that God raised him from the dead, you will be saved." (Romans 10:9 NIV)

Declare, believe. At one level we are already united with every single person who has done those two simple things— whether we like it or not! And we are to maintain that unity.

Does that mean agreement on doctrine? When churches believed that, the outcome was split after split after painful split.

Yet good doctrine is important. The Bible is the Word of God. The early Church formulated statements of truth to help ensure people understood key elements. One of these early statements is 1 Corinthians 15:3–5. And it's fascinating that it lists just three key things:

- Christ died for our sins according to the Scriptures;
- He was buried;
- He was raised on the third day.

If someone does not believe these *essential* doctrines, it's difficult to imagine that they actually know Jesus at all. But just three things!

It's also good to seek out the truth of God's Word on less essential matters. But, as we've seen, although truth never changes, our *understanding* of truth can change.

If we insist that our current understanding of a nonessential doctrine is better than someone else's, we are no longer walking in love, but in pride. We are valuing a difference more than we value our relationship with our brothers and sisters in Christ.

> 100% GRACE AND 100% TRUTH

Jesus came to us "full of grace and truth" (John 1:14). 100% grace and 100% truth.

Every generation faces seemingly intractable issues of doctrine that challenge our unity. Paul addressed the big unity issue in the Church of his day—whether or not to eat food that had been offered to idols—with 100% grace and 100% truth.

He tells Gentile Christians (in 1 Corinthians 8) that it's perfectly okay to eat meat that's been offered to idols—that's the *truth*. But then he follows it up with *grace* and tells them that if they do it in the presence of someone who believes it's not okay, *then* it becomes sin.

The sin is not the eating of the meat, it's wounding the conscience of a brother or sister in Christ who has a different understanding of a nonessential question. The onus is on the person who thinks they have the correct doctrine—which, of course, we all do!—to act with grace toward those who believe something different.

Unless we have really understood God's incredible grace, it's difficult to lay down the pride that makes us want to prove we are right; or the fear that makes us shy away from working with those from other parts of the Body of Christ.

We encourage you to commit to maintain the unity of the Spirit in the bond of peace by using the "Prayer For Unity" on page 106.

> THE WEDDING CELEBRATION

Revelation 7:9 tells us that, at the end of time, "A great multitude that no one could number, from every nation, from all tribes and peoples and languages" will assemble, and there will be a wedding to end all weddings.

And because we know Jesus, we are invited! But we are not *guests* at this wedding, we—the Church—are the bride and will be married to Jesus, the Lamb of God.

As *individual* Christians, we stand with our sandals, our ring, and our robe. But *together* as the Bride of Christ, we, the Church, will be unimaginably glorious.

And God has such confidence in us that in Revelation 19:7, we see in black and white that we, His bride, *will* have made ourselves ready.

Let's live and work together in the grace we have received as we make ourselves ready!

REFLECT

Invite the Holy Spirit to show you any times when you have been arrogant toward other Christians.

Read John 3:17 and then ask the Holy Spirit to show you any times when you have condemned those who do not yet know Jesus.

How can you play your part in helping the Bride prepare herself for Jesus' return?

We invite you to finish this time by speaking out the Prayer for Unity on the next page.

> PRAYER FOR UNITY

Lord Jesus,

We join You in Your prayer to the Father that Your children would be one—because, like You, we want the world to believe that the Father sent You. You have said in Your Word that where there is unity You command a blessing, and we want to see that blessing come in full force. Just as You—the great King of Kings—humbled Yourself by taking the form of a servant, even to the point of choosing to die a humiliating and agonizing death on a cross, we choose to give up our pretensions of being in any way righteous or right in our own strength, and we humble ourselves before You.

It's all about You and Your Kingdom, Lord, and not about us. We choose also to humble ourselves before each other in Christ and to come not just with truth but with grace—just as You come to us. We choose to consider others more important than ourselves and to put their interests above our own. We recognize that without genuine love, anything we do is no more than a noisy gong or clanging cymbal.

Even if our Christian doctrine and tradition are one hundred percent right, without love they are worth nothing.

Lord, we are eager to maintain the unity of the Spirit in the bond of peace. We therefore ask You to fill us afresh with the Holy Spirit and to lead us in love.

We choose to be peacemakers not nitpickers.

We choose relationship above rules.

We choose love above law.

We choose to be real rather than right.

We pray all this in the Name of the humble Jesus, the One who has now been lifted up to the very highest place and who has the Name that is above every other name, Amen.

(Based on Psalm 133; John 1:14–17; John 17:20–23; 1 Corinthians 13; Ephesians 4:1–7; Philippians 2:1–11)

STEPS TO EXPERIENCING GOD'S GRACE!

OBJECTIVE

To ask the Holy Spirit to reveal areas where we need to repent so that we can resolve personal and spiritual conflicts, remove "false motivators," and go on to live out of a deep appreciation of God's grace.

FOCUS VERSE

Submit yourselves therefore to God. Resist the devil,
and he will flee from you.

James 4:7

 ### FOCUS TRUTH

Christ has set us free (Galatians 5:1), but we will not experience that freedom without genuine repentance.

Confession (admitting that we did wrong) is the first step to repentance but is not enough on its own. We must both submit to God and resist the devil. We must also make a choice about what we believe and how we are living, and decide to change. If we want to grow in Christ we must choose to renounce the lies we have believed and any sin in our lives, and announce our choice to believe that what God says is true and start to live accordingly.

> INTRODUCTION

This kind, gentle process of prayer and repentance is for every Christian who wants to grow in Christ, learn to live the "grace-rest" life, and bear fruit that will last for eternity. God the Father offers you an invitation to come "home," just as the father in the story of the prodigal son did. *The Steps To Experiencing God's Grace* will enable you to affirm your love for God, and allow Him to point out areas in your life that need some attention. If you feel distant from God, if your Christian walk has become a heavy, dull, lifeless burden, or if you are losing hope that you will ever break free from slavery to sin or fear, these Steps will be especially helpful. They will help you take hold of who you are and what you have in Christ to live in God's grace where there is genuine "rest for your soul"—a different way to live!

The "grace-rest life" could look like this:

- You live for God and show love to others because of the love you yourself have received from Him and not for any other reason.

- You experience daily victory over temptation as a consequence of the power of the Holy Spirit within you, rather than any power or effort you have to exert.

- You find yourself becoming abundantly fruitful, bringing God much glory, by staying in a dependent relationship of rest in Him.

When we begin to see our lives from His perspective, it can be painful to realize just how far we may have wandered away from Father God. Remember, as we return to that place of experiencing grace, God does not require us to try harder to please Him. Quite the opposite, for it was this "slaving away" that kept the elder son at a distance from the father.

Returning to our Father begins with having a change of mind (what the Bible calls "repentance"), committing ourselves to confessing and rejecting lies we have believed, and choosing instead to believe what is really true (as revealed in His Word, the Bible) about who He is, who we now are in Christ, and the circumstances of our lives.

We encourage you to allow the Holy Spirit to reveal not only actions, but also attitudes and false beliefs that have kept you from living in the daily reality of God's grace and producing fruit that will last forever. We recommend that you make a note of any false beliefs and lies that you become aware of during the process in the Lies List at the end of this book. We will explain how to replace these with truth using "stronghold-busting" so that you can renew your mind and be transformed (Romans 12:2).

Striving for acceptance from God or others through performing well can look very spiritual on the outside. But it reveals beliefs that misrepresent who God is and who we are. It may not be obvious to others from your actions that there is anything amiss, because your external behavior itself may not look that different from that of those who are living in the experience of grace. But *inside* there is all the difference in the world. Remember, God looks inside at the heart. Thankfully, in Christ we have all been given a brand-new heart!

Throughout this process we will depend completely on the Holy Spirit, whose role is to lead us into all truth, so that we can take hold of the freedom God has given us as His precious children and offer our whole selves back to Him in love and gratitude, knowing that He "is able to do far more abundantly than all that we ask or think, according to the power at work within us" (Ephesians 3:20).

To begin, take a moment to remind yourself of who God is and what He has done and praise Him.

Then, when you are ready, say the prayer and declaration on the next pages aloud.

> OPENING PRAYER

Dear Heavenly Father,

I thank You that You love me and that Your Son died and rose again so that I could have an intimate relationship with You. I want to live my life on the basis of Your acceptance of me and relate to You not only through head knowledge, but also through true heart experience. Your Word says it was "for freedom Christ has set us free" (Galatians 5:1), and I ask You to help me take hold of that freedom today. There are many ways in which I have not stood firm in Your new covenant of grace, but instead have allowed a yoke of slavery to weigh me down and wear me out. Please help me take hold of my freedom from all slavery to sin, fear, or performance. Please bring to my mind all the attitudes and actions that have kept me from receiving and giving away Your love. Help me to know the truth so that I will be set free to love You and others in the way that You love me. In Jesus' name I pray. Amen.

(Prayer 1.A)

> OPENING DECLARATION

In the name and authority of the Lord Jesus Christ, I command Satan and all evil spirits to release me, in order that I can be free to know and choose to do the will of God. As a child of God seated with Christ in the heavenly places, I agree that every enemy of the Lord Jesus Christ be bound to silence. I say to Satan and all your evil workers that you cannot inflict any pain or in any way prevent God's will from being accomplished in my life. I belong to God and the evil one cannot touch me. I refuse all fear, anxiety, doubt, confusion, deception, distraction, and any other interference that comes from the enemies of the Lord Jesus Christ. I choose to take my place in Christ, and I declare that all His enemies have been disarmed, and that Jesus Himself came to destroy the devil's work in my life. I declare that the chains of bondage have already been broken by Christ and that I am in Him. Therefore His victory is my victory.

(Declaration 1.B)

STEP ONE: CHOOSING TO BELIEVE THE TRUTH

In this first Step we will affirm some key truths from the Bible. It is important to reject all the lies you have become aware of during *The Grace Course* and instead choose to declare and believe what is actually true according to God's Word. God may also use the affirmations to reveal more faulty thinking to you.

Start by praying the following prayer aloud:

Dear Heavenly Father,

Your Word is truth and Jesus Himself is the Truth. The Holy Spirit is the Spirit of truth and it is knowing the truth that will set me free. I want to know the truth, believe the truth, and live in accordance with the truth. Please reveal to my mind all the lies I have believed about You, my Father God, and about myself, Your beloved child. I want to renounce those lies and walk in the truth of Your grace and Your acceptance of me in Christ. In Jesus' name I pray. Amen.

(Prayer 1.C)

> THE TRUTH ABOUT OUR FATHER GOD

Having a wrong view of God's character and His expectations of us will hinder the development of a close intimate relationship with Him. These declarations about your Father God will give you an opportunity to renounce out loud the lies you have believed about God, and to affirm the truth about His character. We encourage you to do this boldly, especially for those truths that seem hard to receive for you today. Meditating on the truth of who God is can be one of the most important aspects of your freedom and healing in Christ.

Declare out loud all of the statements on the next two pages.

I reject the lie that You, Father God, are distant and uninterested in me.

I choose to believe the truth that You, Father God, are always personally present with me, have plans to give me a hope and a future, and have prepared works in advance specifically for me to do.

(Psalm 139:1–18; Matthew 28:20; Jeremiah 29:11; Ephesians 2:10)

I reject the lie that You, Father God, are insensitive and don't know me or care for me.

I choose to believe the truth that You, Father God, are kind and compassionate and know every single thing about me.

(Psalm 103:8–14; 1 John 3:1–3; Hebrews 4:12–13)

I reject the lie that You, Father God, are stern and have placed unrealistic expectations on me.

I choose to believe the truth that You, Father God, have accepted me and are joyfully supportive of me.

(Romans 15:7; Zephaniah 3:17)

I reject the lie that You, Father God, are passive and cold toward me.

I choose to believe the truth that You, Father God, are warm and affectionate toward me.

(Isaiah 40:11; Hosea 11:3–4)

I reject the lie that You, Father God, are absent or too busy for me.

I choose to believe the truth that You, Father God, are always present and eager to be with me and enable me to be all that You created me to be.

(Philippians 1:6; Hebrews 13:5)

I reject the lie that You, Father God, are impatient or angry with me, or have rejected me.

I choose to believe the truth that You, Father God, are patient and slow to anger, and that when You discipline me, it is a proof of Your love, and not rejection.

(Exodus 34:6; Romans 2:4; Hebrews 12:5–11)

I reject the lie that You, Father God, have been mean, cruel, or abusive to me.

I choose to believe the truth that Satan is mean, cruel, and abusive, but You, Father God, are loving, gentle, and protective.

(Psalm 18:2; Matthew 11:28–30; Ephesians 6:10–18)

I reject the lie that You, Father God, are denying me the pleasures of life.

I choose to believe the truth that You, Father God, are the author of life and will lead me into love, joy, and peace when I choose to be filled with Your Spirit.

(Lamentations 3:22–23; Galatians 5:22–24)

I reject the lie that You, Father God, are trying to control and manipulate me.

I choose to believe the truth that You, Father God, have set me free, and give me the freedom to make choices and grow in Your grace.

(Galatians 5:1; Hebrews 4:15–16)

I reject the lie that You, Father God, have condemned me, and no longer forgive me.

I choose to believe the truth that You, Father God, have forgiven all my sins and will never use them against me in the future.

(Jeremiah 31:31–34; Romans 8:1)

I reject the lie that You, Father God, reject me when I fail to live a perfect or sinless life.

I choose to believe the truth that You, Father God, are patient toward me and cleanse me when I fail.

(Proverbs 24:16; 1 John 1:7–2:2)

I AM THE APPLE OF YOUR EYE!
(Deuteronomy 32:9–10)

(Declaration 1.D)

Now look back over the list and mark any truths that you find difficult to believe. You can use the "Stronghold-Busting" process outlined at the end of the *Steps* to ensure that you replace lies with truth. But for now, use the following prayer to affirm those truths about your Father God that you have marked.

Dear Heavenly Father,

I thank You for Your grace and forgiveness. I choose to believe the truth(s) that You are _____ (list the truths). Please change the way I worship, pray, live, and serve in the light of those truths and fill me with Your Holy Spirit. In Jesus' name. Amen.

(Prayer 1.E)

> THE TRUTH ABOUT WHO WE ARE IN CHRIST

The term the Bible most often uses for those who are now in Christ is "holy ones." But we often have the impression that God sees us as "sinners," which is the term most often used in the Bible for those who do not yet know Jesus as their Savior. Because we behave according to how we see ourselves, it is of crucial importance that we understand who God says we are. Remember, we have not earned any of this—our new identity is a pure grace gift from Him. But it is nevertheless true!

Declare out loud the statements below.

I joyfully announce the truth that I am safe and secure in Christ:

I am loved by God as much as He loves Jesus (John 17:23)

I have been purchased by the blood of His Son (1 Corinthians 6:20)

I am connected to Jesus like a branch to the vine (John 15:5)

I am protected and held in Jesus' and the Father's hands (John 10:27–30)

I am the righteousness of God in Christ, therefore in Him I do measure up! (2 Corinthians 5:21)

I died with Christ to the rule of sin and have been raised up to live a new life (Romans 6:3–4)

I died to the law through the body of Christ (Romans 7:4)

I will never be deserted or abandoned by Christ (Hebrews 13:5)

I am my Father's workmanship, His "poem" (Ephesians 2:10)

I joyfully announce the truth that the Holy Spirit lives in me and He is my strength:

I am the Temple of the Holy Spirit, who was given to me by my Father (1 Corinthians 6:19)

I am sealed by the Spirit, who was given to me as a pledge of my full inheritance in Christ (Ephesians 1:13)

I am led by the Spirit of adoption and am no longer a slave to fear; He enables me to cry out "Abba! Father!" (Romans 8:14–15)

I have been baptized by the Holy Spirit and placed into the body of Christ as a full member (1 Corinthians 12:13)

I have been given spiritual gifts by the Holy Spirit (1 Corinthians 12:7, 11)

I can walk by the Holy Spirit instead of giving in to the lusts of my flesh (Galatians 5:16–18, 25)

I am the apple of His eye! (Deuteronomy 32:9–10)

(Declaration 1.F)

Now look back over the list and mark any truths that you find difficult to believe. You can use the "Stronghold-Busting" process outlined at the end of the *Steps* to ensure that you replace lies with truth. But for now, use the following prayer to affirm those truths about yourself that you have marked.

Dear Heavenly Father,

I thank You for Your grace and forgiveness. I choose to believe the truth(s) that I am _____ (list the truths). Please change the way I worship, pray, live, and serve in the light of those truths and fill me with your Holy Spirit. In Jesus' name. Amen.

(Prayer 1.G)

> RECEIVING YOUR NEW NAME

In Session 2 of *The Grace Course* we saw that God has cleansed us from shame, and that He has given us a new name. In fact, there are many names God gives us in the Bible. Here are some of them:

- Beloved (Colossians 3:12)
- Chosen (Ephesians 1:4)
- Precious (Isaiah 43:4)
- Loved (1 John 4:10)
- Clean (John 15:3)
- Presentable (Luke 17:14)
- Protected (Psalm 91:14; John 17:15)
- Welcomed (Ephesians 3:12)
- Heir (Romans 8:17; Galatians 3:29)
- Complete (Colossians 2:10)
- Holy (Hebrews 10:10; Ephesians 1:4)
- Forgiven (Psalm 103:3; Colossians 2:13)
- Adopted (Ephesians 1:5)
- Delight (Psalm 147:11)
- Unashamed (Romans 10:11)

- Known (Psalm 139:1)
- Planned (Ephesians 1:11–12)
- Gifted (2 Timothy 1:6; 1 Corinthians 12:11)
- Enriched (2 Corinthians 8:9)
- Provided For (1 Timothy 6:17)
- Treasured (Deuteronomy 7:6)
- Pure (1 Corinthians 6:11)
- Established (Romans 16:25)
- God's Work of Art (Ephesians 2:10)
- Helped (Hebrews 13:5)
- Free from Condemnation (Romans 8:1)
- God's Child (Romans 8:15)
- Christ's Friend (John 15:15)
- Christ's Precious Bride (Isaiah 54:5; Song of Songs 7:10)

Pray the following prayer:

Dear Heavenly Father,

Thank You that You have given me a new name! Please show me which of these names you particularly want me to take hold of now. In Jesus' name. Amen.

(Prayer 1.H)

For each new name that God is impressing upon you say:

> **Thank You, Father God, that my new name is _____.**
>
> *(Prayer 1.I)*

We strongly encourage you to continue declaring your new name(s) every morning for at least the next 40 days and at other times throughout the day whenever you feel attacked in your mind by the lies of the enemy.

STEP TWO: WALKING BY THE SPIRIT RATHER THAN THE FLESH

Even though we are now new creations in Christ at the deepest level of our beings, we still have a tendency toward sin that the Bible calls "the flesh." Every day we can choose either to walk by the Spirit or by the flesh. In this Step we will invite our Father to show us where we have believed the lies that the flesh feeds us and allowed ourselves to return to slavery to sin.

To begin this Step, say this prayer aloud:

> **Dear Heavenly Father,**
>
> **You have told me in Your Word to "put on the Lord Jesus Christ, and make no provision for the flesh in regard to its lusts" (Romans 13:14 NASB). Thank You that Jesus has not only forgiven my sins but given me the power to overcome sin in my life. I acknowledge, however, that by giving in to temptation, I have given sin the opportunity to reign in my body (Romans 6:12). Please reveal to my mind all the sins of the flesh I have committed so that I may now take hold of my freedom from sin. In Jesus' name. Amen.**
>
> *(Prayer 2.A)*

The following list of sins of the flesh is based on Galatians 5:19–21. Mark any that you need to confess:

- ☐ Sexual sins
- ☐ Drunkenness
- ☐ Other forms of impurity
- ☐ Worship of something other than God
- ☐ Engaging in occult activities
- ☐ Hatred
- ☐ Anger
- ☐ Divisiveness
- ☐ Envy and jealousy
- ☐ Selfish ambition
- ☐ Other sins of the flesh: _____

Dear Heavenly Father,

I confess that I have given in to the flesh and sinned against You in the following ways: _____.

Thank You for Your forgiveness and for Your complete cleansing of me through the blood of Jesus. Thank You that You have made me pure and holy.

I choose no longer to present the parts of my body to sin but instead to present them to You to be used for righteousness.

Thank You that, because I have died with Christ, I have been set free from sin and that, because I have risen with Him, I need never return to being a slave to sin. I declare that I am dead to sin and alive to God in Christ Jesus.

Thank You that You have promised always to provide a way out of temptation—please help me to recognize it and take it. (See 1 Corinthians 10:13.)

I ask You to fill me afresh with Your Holy Spirit and I choose to allow You to develop the fruit of the Spirit in my life, which is "love, joy, peace, patience, kindness, goodness, gentleness, faithfulness and self-control."

In Jesus' name I pray. Amen. (See Galatians 5:22–23.)

(Prayer 2.B)

STEP THREE: PRIDE, PERFORMANCE, AND PERFECTIONISM

The elder brother mistakenly believed that he had to earn anything that would come from his father, but the truth was that he could have been enjoying everything the father had all along. We're going to begin this Step by asking God to reveal to us the expectations, standards, and demands of others that we have felt we need to live up to in order to feel good about ourselves, to measure up, or to be acceptable. Pray the following prayer:

> Loving Father,
>
> I thank You that in Christ all of Your expectations of me have been fully met (Romans 8:4), and that You have forgiven me all my sins and canceled out my certificate of debt by nailing it to the cross (Colossians 2:13–14). I confess that I have believed the lie that I have needed something more than Christ in order to gain or maintain acceptance from You and others.
>
> Please would You reveal to me now all the expectations, standards, and demands that I have been living under, by which I have sought to become more acceptable and feel less guilty, so that I can return in simple faith and rely only on what Jesus has done on my behalf. I ask this in the name of Jesus Christ, who died for me. Amen.
>
> *(Prayer 3.A)*

Now spend time evaluating where you have lived under false expectations and write the false expectations, standards, and demands you have lived under on a separate sheet of paper:

- Expectations you wrongly believed were from God
- Expectations from parents and family
- Expectations from teachers
- Expectations from churches and church leaders
- Expectations from employers
- Other expectations, standards, and demands: _____

Then use the following prayer to reject every false expectation:

I reject the lie that I have to live up to the expectations, standards, and demands of others in order to feel good enough, valued, or accepted. I specifically reject these false expectations: _____.

Thank You, Lord Jesus, that in You I meet all of God's expectations and that nothing I could do could make You love me more or love me less. Amen.

(Prayer 3.B)

You may like to rip up your piece of paper in order to symbolize that you choose from now on to trust in Jesus alone to make you right with God. Then move on in freedom and confidence! Before you do so, make a note of any persistent lies you have believed so that you can address them later with a stronghold-buster.

We will now consider other areas where we have lived our lives in our own strength instead of from a place of rest in what God has done. Say the following prayer aloud:

Dear Lord,

I ask You to reveal to me now the ways in which the sins of performance, perfectionism, pride, power, and pleasureless living have been issues in my life so that I can turn away from them. I want to confess those times that I have lived my life in my own strength rather than resting in You, when I have believed that my ways are better than Your ways or that my preferences are better than those of other people. In Jesus' name. Amen.

(Prayer 3.C)

Consider these potential areas of weakness and mark any actions and attitudes that the Holy Spirit shows you:

PERFORMANCE

- ☐ Centering my life around keeping laws and rules rather than knowing God
- ☐ Trying to keep God's commands in order to gain His acceptance or favor
- ☐ Trying to keep God's commands in my own strength
- ☐ Being driven to work harder and harder in order to achieve
- ☐ Believing achievement is the means of gaining personal happiness and a sense of worth

PERFECTIONISM

- ☐ Living in the fear of failure
- ☐ Being afraid of going to hell because I have not kept God's laws perfectly
- ☐ Being unable to accept God's grace because I think I need to be "punished" even though Jesus paid for all my sins in full on the cross
- ☐ Being obsessed with keeping things in exact order, and being unable to experience joy and satisfaction when life is not perfect
- ☐ Being overly concerned or punishing others with minor flaws and/or having unreasonable expectations of perfection
- ☐ Being angry at others when they disrupt my neatly controlled world and/or resisting new ideas

PRIDE AND JUDGMENTALISM

- ☐ Thinking I am more spiritual, devoted, humble, or devout than others
- ☐ Thinking that my church, denomination, or group is better than others
- ☐ Not being willing to associate with others who are different (having an independent spirit)
- ☐ Not being willing to tolerate different religious opinions on nonessentials (e.g., baptism, communion, end times theology, etc.) in order to promote love, peace, and unity among true brothers and sisters in Christ
- ☐ Finding it hard to admit that I am wrong, or wanting to prove that I am right
- ☐ Criticizing Christian ministers and leaders
- ☐ Judging others' motives and character or labeling others

POWER AND CONTROL

- ☐ Experiencing anxiety when I am not able to be in control
- ☐ Finding security in rules, regulations, and standards rather than in the Lord
- ☐ Being more concerned about controlling others (by means of strong personality, overbearing persuasion, fear, or intimidation) than developing self-control

☐ Being driven to attain positions of power or accomplish my own agenda

☐ Feeling unhealthy responsibility for the lives and well-being of others

☐ Using guilt and shame tactics to get others to do what I want or think is best

PLEASURELESS LIVING

☐ Living a joyless life of duty and obligation

☐ Feeling guilty for experiencing pleasure or being secretive in pursuing it

☐ Being unable to relax and rest

☐ Being strongly attracted to (or giving in to) illegal substances, illicit sex, pornography, etc., in order to escape or to find some gratification

Use the prayer below to confess and renounce aloud those things the Holy Spirit has revealed to you:

> Dear Heavenly Father,
>
> I confess that I have _____ (name the items you marked).
>
> I agree that these attitudes and actions do not reflect who I truly am in Christ and I renounce them all. I turn away from living in my own strength according to my own ideas and choose now to adopt the same attitude You had and humble myself before You and before other people. I declare the truth that Your ways are higher than my ways. I declare that I am in no way better than other people, and I choose to consider others as more significant than myself.
>
> Thank You for Your forgiveness. Thank You that, because I know I am Your child, I no longer have to lift myself up but can rely on You to lift me up in due course. In Jesus' holy name I pray. Amen.
>
> *(Prayer 3.D)*

In order to make a permanent change to your thinking, you will need to renew your mind. You will find stronghold-busting helpful for this.

STEP FOUR: FORGIVING OTHERS

Experiencing God's forgiveness in your own life frees you to forgive others.

The pain we feel in our lives because of the physical, verbal, emotional, sexual, or spiritual abuse we have suffered can be devastating. It is a very human thing to experience anger toward those who have hurt or offended us; Jesus Christ can enter into those wounded places and begin to heal the damage done to our souls and free us from the hold they have over us. The healing begins when we make a choice to forgive from our hearts.

We may also need to forgive ourselves for wrong choices we have made, as well as surrender our false beliefs about God's character.

To forgive means:

- Choosing not to hold someone's sin against them any more.

- Canceling their debt and letting them off our hook, knowing that they are not off God's hook and that He will make everything right in the end.

- Releasing the person and what they did into God's hands and resolving not to bring the offense up in conversation any more.

- Trusting Him to deal with that person justly—something we are not able to do.

- Letting go of the right to seek revenge.

Holding on to your anger hurts you more than it hurts them. If you want to be free, you need to forgive them from your heart. Forgiving someone from the heart simply means being honest both with God and yourself about how what was done to you made you feel. Allow Jesus to bring to the surface the feelings that you have held inside for so long, so that He can begin to heal those emotional hurts and pain.

Begin by saying the following prayer aloud:

Dear Heavenly Father,

Thank You for the riches of Your grace, kindness, and patience toward me, knowing that Your kindness has led me to repentance. Please show me all the people I need to forgive, including myself. Show me too where in my suffering I have believed lies about You. In Jesus' name I pray. Amen. (See Romans 2:4.)

(Prayer 4.A)

Make a list (by name if possible) of all those the Holy Spirit brings to your mind, which could include

- **Anyone** who was used by the enemy to rob me of freedom and joy, including any perpetrators of abuse or neglect, or who caused me to believe I was worthless, unlovable, or valuable only when I "performed well."

- **Anyone** who stifled the free expression of grace or spiritual liberty in my life and who forced me to conform to unattainable standards.

- **Parents, church leaders, school teachers, or officials** who were harsh, critical, or judgmental and who fostered a performance-based rather than a grace-based environment.

- **Myself** for imposing on myself heavy burdens and thus robbing myself of freedom and joy.

- **God Himself**—It is vital for our freedom that we acknowledge and turn away from any false beliefs we have developed about God's character because of what He has allowed in our lives, even though we may not understand why He allowed it. The truth is He has done no wrong, and has never left us or abandoned us. He promises to work all things together for our good (Hebrews 13:5; Romans 8:28). We can receive His grace afresh and put our trust in Him again.

When you are ready, start wherever you want on your list, and begin to forgive from your heart those people who have hurt you, whether they did it deliberately or not. Take your time and be sure to be honest with God by telling Him every painful memory and how they made you feel.

Dear Heavenly Father,

I choose to forgive _____ (the name of the person or group) for _____ (be specific in what they did or failed to do), which made me feel _____ (be honest in expressing how you felt or still feel.)

(Prayer 4.B)

Once you have forgiven all those on your list, pray a blessing on each of them (including yourself):

> **Dear Heavenly Father,**
>
> **I choose no longer to seek revenge or to hold on to my bitterness toward _____ (name). Thank You for setting me free from the bondage of my bitterness. I now ask You to bless _____ (name). In Jesus' name. Amen.**
>
> *(Prayer 4.C)*

A PRAYER TO RELEASE GOD FROM UNFULFILLED EXPECTATIONS

If you realize that you have had angry thoughts toward God, say this prayer aloud:

> **Dear Heavenly Father, I release You from my unfulfilled expectations and the secret anger and bitterness I have held against You. I reject the lie that You are like those who have failed me, and I declare the truth that You love me with an everlasting love. I now bless You. Amen.**
>
> *(Prayer 4.D)*

We recommend that you consider taking another look at what you said after "which made me feel" in Prayer 4.B above. If you find the same word or expression repeated two or three times, it may indicate a false belief that you hold that you can deal with using the "stronghold-busting" process.

STEP FIVE: FREEDOM FROM FEAR

In this Step we will be asking God to reveal any unhealthy fears. An unhealthy fear is something that we wrongly believe is both present and powerful.

Begin by saying the following prayer out loud:

Dear Heavenly Father,

I come to You as Your child and acknowledge that You are the only legitimate fear object in my life. I confess that I have been fearful and anxious because of my lack of trust and unbelief in Your protective care. I have not always lived by faith in You and too often I have relied on my own strength and resources. I thank You that I am forgiven in Christ. I choose to believe the truth that You have not given me a spirit of fear, but of power, love, and a sound mind (2 Timothy 1:7). Therefore, I reject any spirit of fear. I ask You to reveal to my mind all the unhealthy fears that have been controlling me. Show me how I have become fearful and the lies I have believed. Open the eyes of my heart to Your wonderful truths. I desire to live a responsible life in the power of Your Holy Spirit. Show me how these fears have kept me from doing that. I ask this so that I can confess, reject, and overcome every fear by faith in You. In Jesus' name. Amen.

(Prayer 5.A)

The following list may help you recognize some of the unhealthy fears that have been hindering your walk of faith. Mark the ones that apply to you, as well as any others not on the list that the Spirit of God has revealed to you.

- ☐ Fear of Satan
- ☐ Fear of death or the death of a loved one
- ☐ Fear of not being loved by God
- ☐ Fear of the future
- ☐ Fear of financial problems
- ☐ Fear of losing my mind or of being a hopeless case
- ☐ Fear of never getting married
- ☐ Fear of never having children
- ☐ Fear of not being able to love others

- ☐ Fear of rejection/disapproval/embarrassment
- ☐ Fear of marriage or divorce
- ☐ Fear of failure
- ☐ Fear of confrontation
- ☐ Fear of being a victim of crime
- ☐ Fear of having committed the unpardonable sin
- ☐ Fear of specific animals or objects
- ☐ Other unhealthy fears_____

Remember, behind every unhealthy fear is a lie. It will help you hugely if you are able to identify these lies, because renouncing them and choosing the truth is a critical step toward gaining and maintaining your freedom in Christ. You have to **know** and choose to **believe** the truth in order for it to set you free.

When you are ready, use the following table (or a separate piece of paper) to write down the unhealthy fear. Then work out the lie behind the fear and the corresponding truths from the Word of God. This is not easy because the lies seem true and have probably been with you a long time. If you can, get some help from a mature Christian friend.

FEAR	LIE	TRUTH
Example: failure	If I fail it will make me worthless	"I am precious in His sight and He loves me" (see Isaiah 43:4).

Express the following prayer for each of the controlling fears that you have identified:

Dear Father,

I confess and repent of the fear of _____. I have believed_____ (state the lie). I reject that lie and I choose to believe the truth _____ (state the truth). I also confess any and all ways this fear has resulted in living irresponsibly, or compromising my witness for Christ. I now choose to believe Your promise that You will protect me and meet all my needs as I live by faith in You (Psalm 23:1; 27:1; Matthew 6:33–34). In Jesus' trustworthy name. Amen.

(Prayer 5.B)

FEAR OF PEOPLE

Proverbs 29:25 says, "Fear of man will prove to be a snare, but whoever trusts in the LORD is kept safe" (NIV). Fearing people ultimately leads to pleasing people—and that indeed is bondage. People-pleasers find themselves more and more concerned about what others around them think, because they wrongly believe that their personal worth and happiness are dependent upon the acceptance or approval of others.

When we make it our goal to keep people happy, we end up becoming enslaved to them and we remove ourselves from the safety and security of serving Christ alone (Galatians 1:10). To allow the Holy Spirit to examine your heart in this area, begin by praying:

Dear Heavenly Father,

I know that I have not always walked by faith but have allowed the fear of people to control me. I have been too concerned about gaining approval from others, and I have been led astray from a simple, pure devotion to Christ. I want to walk in a healthy fear and awe of You and not of people. Thank You for Your forgiveness. I now ask You to bring to my mind the specific ways that I have allowed the fear of other people to control me. In Jesus' name I pray. Amen.

(Prayer 5.C)

Now mark on the following list areas that the Holy Spirit is revealing to you:

☐ I constantly need the affirmation of other people in order to feel happy, significant, or worthwhile and can easily become depressed and discouraged and give up.

☐ I have been afraid to say what I really think or feel for fear of being reprimanded, ridiculed, or rejected.

☐ I am afraid to say no when asked to do something for fear of experiencing disapproval or anger, and I am often tired, on the verge of burn-out, or feeling used.

☐ I can't seem to bring myself to set healthy boundaries in my life.

☐ I find myself easily intimidated by strong personalities.

☐ I don't handle criticism well; it is painful because it makes me feel like a failure.

☐ I make sure that others know about the "good" things I have done.

☐ I have found myself lying in order to cover things up in my life that might result in disapproval from others.

☐ I have been more concerned with following human traditions in our church than with obeying God's Word.

☐ Other ways I have allowed the fear of others to control me_____.

Now use this prayer to confess your fear of people:

Dear Heavenly Father,

Thank You for showing me how my life has been influenced by the fear of people, and how I have tried to please them rather than You. I specifically confess _____ (list the areas that the Holy Spirit revealed to you).

Thank You for Your gracious forgiveness and that You already love, accept, and approve of me, so I don't have to go looking for those things in other people. You are indeed trustworthy, so I choose to believe You, even when my feelings and circumstances tell me to fear. You are always with me and You will strengthen me, help me, and uphold me with Your righteous right hand.

Teach me what pleases You, regardless of others' opinions. I trust in Your power within me to walk in awe of You alone. In Jesus' mighty name. Amen. (See Isaiah 41:10.)

(Prayer 5.D)

STEP SIX: EXCHANGING ANXIETY FOR GOD'S PEACE

Paul said, "Do not be anxious about anything, but in everything by prayer and supplication with thanksgiving let your requests be made known to God" (Philippians 4:6). He also told us to cast our anxiety onto Christ, who cares for us (1 Peter 5:7). In this Step we will put into practice the principles we learned about casting our anxiety onto Christ in Session 6 of *The Grace Course*.

Prayer is the first step in casting all your anxiety on Christ. Ask God to guide you by saying the following prayer aloud:

> **Dear Heavenly Father,**
>
> **As Your child I declare my dependence upon You, and I acknowledge my need for You. I know that apart from Christ I can do nothing.**
>
> **You know the thoughts and intentions of my heart, and You know the situation I am in from the beginning to the end. I do not want to be double-minded and need Your peace to guard my heart and my mind.**
>
> **I place my trust in You to supply all my needs according to Your riches in glory and to guide me into all truth. I ask for Your guidance so that I may fulfill my calling to live a responsible life by faith in the power of Your Holy Spirit.**
>
> **Search me, O God, and know my heart. Test me and know my anxious thoughts. Point out anything in me that offends You, and lead me along the path of everlasting life. In Jesus' precious name. Amen. (See Psalm 139:23–24.)**
>
> *(Prayer 6.A)*

You are responsible only for that which you have the right and ability to control. You are not responsible for that which you don't. Your sense of worth should be tied only to that for which you are responsible.

If you aren't living a responsible life, you should feel anxious! Don't try to cast your *responsibility* onto Christ—He will throw it back to you. But do cast your *anxiety* onto Him because His integrity is at stake in meeting your needs if you are living a responsible and righteous life. State the problem—what is making you anxious?

Use this table prayerfully to examine what you are anxious about:

State the problem	What are the facts of the situation?	What assumptions am I making?	What can I control and what is my responsibility?
Example: I've discovered a growth on my arm.	The growth is getting larger.	It's going to be cancerous and my arm will be amputated.	To take my thoughts captive. To pray and seek wise medical help.

The rest is God's responsibility. Your only remaining responsibility is to continue to pray and focus on the truth according to Philippians 4:6–8. Any residual anxiety is due to your assuming responsibilities that God never intended you to have.

Assume responsibility for what is yours to do by praying the following:

Dear Heavenly Father,

Thank You for helping me bring the situations that make me anxious into the light. I turn away from making assumptions and from now on choose to fix my mind on what I know to be the facts of the situation. I turn away from trying to deal with things that are not my responsibility but commit myself to doing the things that are my responsibility. On that basis I cast my anxiety onto You, confident that You will deal with these situations in Your infinite love and wisdom. I leave them with You. In Jesus' mighty name. Amen.

(Prayer 6.B)

A FIVE-DAY WORKOUT TO COMBAT ANXIETY

You may find this exercise helpful in the following days.

Day 1

Practice appreciation for what God has done for you, His child. Look up and read the Bible verses for some of the statements of *The Truth About Who We Are In Christ* in Step One above. Take one and spend time thanking Him for what it means to you.

Day 2

Practice appreciation for who God is using *The Truth About Our Father God* list in Step One. Pick one truth and ask God to remind you of how He has shown Himself to be true to this character quality. Write a prayer to thank Him. Share it with someone else.

Day 3

Think back through each season of your life. Thank God for His grace gifts. Thank Him too for an unanswered prayer—can you now see how He has used it for good? Share one grace gift and a thanksgiving for an unanswered prayer with someone else.

Day 4

Dwell in stories of people in the Bible who overcame fear and anxiety. Read one of the stories below. Where do you see similarities to your story? How did God come through? What characteristics of your Heavenly Father do you see in the outcome?

- Moses (Exodus 3:1–9)

- Elijah—when the evil Jezebel desired to pursue and kill him (1 Kings 19)

- Joseph—His brothers plotted to kill him but instead sold him into slavery. Isn't this the enemy's plan for all of us? Read the outcome in Genesis 39:2–4, 21–23, and 50:19–21.

- Paul (2 Corinthians 4:7–11)

Day 5

Read the Bible verse(s) for some of the new names that you have because of being "in Christ," from Session 2 of *The Grace Course*. How is God working out one today in your life? What would life look like if you really took hold of your new name? Thank God that He has given you a future and a hope. Journal and share with another.

STEP SEVEN: SURRENDERING AS A LIVING SACRIFICE

Are you now ready to make a commitment to God to love Him with an undivided heart, not because you are in any way compelled to, but simply out of love? It is a scary thing to think about surrendering ourselves as a living sacrifice and putting ourselves unreservedly into the hands of another—even if it is God. But remember that He has already shown the depth of His commitment to us by dying for us. In fact, when we surrender ourselves fully into the hands of our loving Father, we are putting ourselves in the only place where we are completely secure.

As children of God, we have the promises that "To all who did receive him, who believed in his name, he gave the right to become children of God" (John 1:12) and "All things belong to you, and you belong to Christ, and Christ belongs to God" (1 Corinthians 3:22–23 NASB). When we lose (surrender) who we are naturally, we discover who we really are in Christ.

To begin this Step, say the following prayer:

> **Dear Heavenly Father,**
>
> **I acknowledge that You are the God who is love and that You have always been faithful to me and will continue to be true to who You are, regardless of my circumstances or how I feel (Lamentations 3:22–23).**
>
> **I confess that I have not always trusted that You have my best interests at heart, or that You can be relied upon to come through on Your promises. I repent of any doubts I may have had concerning Your character and all the ways I have tried to take my life into my own hands.**
>
> **Please show me all the areas where I have held my life back from You. I now ask You to help me take a step of greater trust and dependence on You by surrendering all I am and all I have to You. In Jesus' name. Amen.**
>
> *(Prayer 7.A)*

What do you specifically need to surrender to God now?

- ☐ Living my life in my own strength and resources
- ☐ Saying what I want to say when I want to say it
- ☐ Going where I want to go whenever I please
- ☐ Living wherever I want to live

- ☐ Having the kind of job or house I want
- ☐ Having the kind of financial security I desire
- ☐ Being single or married
- ☐ Having the number (and gender) of children I want to have
- ☐ Having all of my children grow up to love and walk with the Lord
- ☐ Being in control or right all the time
- ☐ Always being loved, accepted, and understood and having a good reputation
- ☐ Having the friends I want
- ☐ Being used by God in specific ways
- ☐ Knowing the will of God all the time
- ☐ Being able to "fix" people or circumstances around me
- ☐ Having good health and being free from pain or suffering
- ☐ Having a specific idea of what a "successful" Christian ministry looks like
- ☐ Receiving forgiveness from those that I have hurt
- ☐ Being spared heartache, crisis, and tragedy
- ☐ Acting in anger toward, or in rebellion against, those who have hurt me
- ☐ Other things the Holy Spirit is laying on my heart: _____

Now pray the following prayer of surrender:

Dear Heavenly Father,

I choose to surrender myself unreservedly to You just as Jesus surrendered Himself for me. I specifically surrender the things you have shown me: _____ . I take my hands off them.

I give You permission to do in me and through me whatever You desire, and whatever will glorify You. Place me wherever You want to place me. Use me however You choose to use me. May Your will be done in me.

I joyfully accept my responsibility to follow Your good, pleasing, and perfect will for me by the power of the Holy Spirit. In Jesus' name I pray. Amen.

(Prayer 7.B)

> CONCLUDING PRAYER

In this final prayer of surrender, we invite you to offer yourself to God as a living and holy sacrifice. You will also complete the process of submitting to God and resisting the devil by commanding every enemy to leave your presence.

Dear Heavenly Father,

As Your redeemed child, I have been bought out of slavery to sin, guilt, shame, and obeying rules. Thank You that because of Christ, the law of God has been written on my heart and mind. I now submit myself to You as an instrument of righteousness, a living and holy sacrifice who will glorify You.

Having submitted to You, I resist the devil, and I command every spiritual enemy of the Lord Jesus Christ to leave my presence.

Father, please fill me with Your Holy Spirit. I commit myself daily to taking every thought captive and renewing my mind. I choose to be motivated by love and nothing else. Thank You that I now live in the grace, forgiveness, acceptance, peace, and rest that are mine in the Lord Jesus Christ. Amen.

(Prayer 7.C)

FINAL AFFIRMATIONS

As a final act of faith, make these declarations out loud to affirm some astonishing biblical truths concerning God's truly amazing grace:

I affirm that God's Word to me is, "Grace to you and peace from God our Father and the Lord Jesus Christ." (Galatians 1:3)

I affirm that it was for freedom that Christ has set me free. I therefore choose to keep standing firm and no longer be subject to the yoke of slavery. (Galatians 5:1)

I affirm that the purpose of the Law was to show me my need for Christ, but now that faith has come I am no longer under the Law. (Galatians 3:24–25)

I affirm that I am now an unconditionally loved, accepted, and secure child of God in Christ. (Galatians 3:26; Ephesians 1:5–6)

I affirm that I am now dead to the Law through the body of Christ and that I have been joined to the risen Christ in order to bear much fruit for God. (Romans 7:4)

I affirm that I am a living sacrifice through Jesus Christ and that my life's purpose is to please Him, not others. (Galatians 1:10)

I affirm that God's strength is now made perfect in my weakness and that His grace is sufficient for me. (2 Corinthians 12:9)

I affirm that, having begun by the Spirit, I am not going to finish through the flesh, but through the transforming power of the Spirit of freedom. (Galatians 3:3; 2 Corinthians 3:17–18)

Therefore I affirm that by the grace of God I am what I am and that by His grace I stand. (1 Corinthians 15:10; Romans 5:2)

All to the praise of His glorious grace, which He freely bestowed on me in Christ. (Ephesians 1:6)

(Final Affirmations 7.D)

STRONGHOLD-BUSTING

OBJECTIVE

To be equipped with a practical approach to replacing faulty beliefs with truth from God's Word so that we can make transformation a way of life.

FOCUS VERSE

Do not conform to the pattern of this world, but be transformed by the renewing of your mind. Then you will be able to test and approve what God's will is—his good, pleasing and perfect will.

Romans 12:2 NIV

 ## FOCUS TRUTH

All of us have ingrained ways of thinking that are not in line with God's truth. Our success in continuing to walk in freedom and grow in maturity depends on the extent to which we renew our minds by uncovering these lies and replacing them with the truth from God's Word.

 ## CONNECT

What is the best practical joke you have experienced?

When Jesus promises that we will know the truth and that the truth will set us free, He speaks as the One who also says that He *is* the Truth. What does it mean to you that Jesus actually *is* the Truth?

PRAYER & DECLARATION

Heavenly Father, thank You that the grace You showed us when Jesus went to the cross is available to us day by day. We pray today that You will guide us into all truth, reveal to us the strongholds in our minds, and help us to renew our minds, so that we will be transformed. We want to be disciples who bear much fruit. We choose to set our hope fully on the grace to be given to us when Jesus Christ is revealed. In His name. Amen.

WE DECLARE THAT, EVEN THOUGH WE LIVE IN THE WORLD, WE DO NOT WAGE WAR AS THE WORLD DOES—WE FIGHT WITH WEAPONS WHICH HAVE DIVINE POWER! FOR EVERY UNHELPFUL WAY OF THINKING THAT HAS A "STRONG HOLD" ON US, WE CHOOSE TO BELIEVE GOD'S CLEAR PROMISE THAT WE CAN DEMOLISH THEM. NOT JUST COPE WITH THEM, WORK AROUND THEM, OR DO THEM A BIT OF DAMAGE. DEMOLISH THEM! AND IN SO DOING WE WILL BE TRANSFORMED BY THE RENEWING OF OUR MINDS.

WORD

WHAT ARE STRONGHOLDS?

Therefore, I urge you, brothers and sisters, in view of God's mercy, to offer your bodies as a living sacrifice, holy and pleasing to God—this is your true and proper worship. Do not conform to the pattern of this world, but be transformed by the renewing of your mind. Then you will be able to test and approve what God's will is—his good, pleasing and perfect will. (Romans 12:1–2 NIV)

We are transformed by the renewing of our mind. "Stronghold-busting" is a very practical way to do that.

The literal meaning of *stronghold* is a fortress, a strong defensive building. But on one occasion in the New Testament, Paul uses it as a metaphor:

For though we live in the world, we do not wage war as the world does. The weapons we fight with are not the weapons of the world. On the contrary, they have divine power to demolish strongholds. We demolish arguments and every pretension that sets itself up against the knowledge of God, and we take captive every thought to make it obedient to Christ. (2 Corinthians 10:3–5 NIV)

The context of this passage is our mind, our thinking. And the word *stronghold* refers to a faulty belief (one that is incompatible with what God says in the Bible) that is deeply ingrained.

Demolishing strongholds and taking every thought captive are not things that God will do for us—they are our responsibility.

Ephesians 2:2–3 says we all "followed the ways of this world and of the ruler of the kingdom of the air, the spirit who is now at work in those who are disobedient. All of us also lived among them . . . following its . . . thoughts" (NIV). Colossians 2:8 tells us not to be taken "captive through hollow and deceptive philosophy, . . . human tradition and the . . . spiritual forces of this world" (NIV).

Perhaps it started out back in childhood when a little thought was planted in your mind by something that happened to you—maybe you were bullied, or someone said something negative about you: "You're useless," "You're a failure," "You're ugly," "It's all your fault."

Later on, the enemy lined up someone else who said or did the same thing. Since he knows your particular vulnerabilities, he ruthlessly exploits them by lining up people or circumstances one after the other to give you the same wrong message.

The world then adds insult to injury with its constant bombardment of lies about what it means to be successful or happy or loved.

And as it gets stronger and stronger, it becomes part of our default thinking and works itself out in our behavior. Perhaps, whenever someone suggests we could go for a particular job or lead a small group at church, a voice plays in our mind, "I couldn't do that. I'm useless at that." We've believed it for so long it has become part of our lives, and we can't imagine it ever being any different.

Feelings of inferiority, insecurity, and inadequacy are all strongholds. Because no child of God is inferior, insecure, or inadequate.

Is any child of God dirty or ugly? Absolutely not. It isn't true. It just *feels* true. It's a lie that's been reinforced so many times that it literally gets a *strong hold* on you and causes you to think and act in ways that contradict God's Word.

PAUSE FOR THOUGHT

1. When we talk about a "lie" on *The Grace Course*, we are referring to a belief that is not in line with what God says in His Word, the Bible. It may feel true but God says it is not true. Here is a list of common lies that people come to believe about themselves:

   • Unloved

   • Rejected

   • Inadequate

   • Hopeless

   • Stupid

   If you are comfortable to do so, share with the group a lie that you realize you have believed. (It does not have to be on the list, of course.)

2. For each lie that has been mentioned—or for the lies on the list—find a Bible verse to show that it is not true of any Christian.

DEMOLISHING STRONGHOLDS

They may have that strong hold on us, but God's clear promise is that we do not have to put up with strongholds—we can demolish them.

This is your responsibility. Nobody else can renew your mind for you. And God won't do it either—in His wisdom and grace it's something that He gives you the responsibility *and* ability to do. So, if you don't do it, it's not going to get done. And there'll be no lasting transformation.

It takes time. Removing the footholds of the enemy that we've given him through sin by going through *The Steps To Freedom In Christ* or *The Steps To Experiencing God's Grace* can be done in a day. But busting a stronghold takes time, several weeks in fact. You will need to persevere—but it will be more than worth it.

By definition the lies you believe *feel* absolutely true. It requires humility and intentionality to bring your thoughts into the light of God's truth.

It's very difficult to demolish a stronghold if you haven't first closed any doors in your life that are open to the enemy through unresolved sin.

Once you've done that, a mental stronghold is simply a habit that can be broken. And creating and using a "stronghold-buster" is a great way to break the habit.

STRONGHOLD-BUSTING

See "Stronghold-Busting Summary" on pages 150–151 and the examples on pages 152–156.

First, identify the faulty belief you want to change, the lie that you now realize is contrary to God's Word.

Next, think about what effect believing that lie is having in your life. Realizing the negative effects will spur us on to tear the stronghold down.

Third, find the truth from God's Word that counteracts the lie. You can use a concordance, a Bible app, or a wise friend to help you find verses that speak truth opposing the lie you believe.

For example, your past experiences may have left you with a sense that you are helpless and that it would be hopeless to try to change. If someone tries to tell you it's a lie, you even respond by thinking, "No, it's true." But turn to your Bible. What does it say?

- Hebrews 13:5 says God will never leave you or forsake you.
- Philippians 4:13 says you can do all things through Him who gives you strength.
- Romans 8:37 says you are more than victorious through Jesus, who loves you.
- 2 Peter 1:3 says God's divine power has given you everything you need for life and godliness.

Next write a declaration:

I refuse to believe the lie that I am hopeless and will never change.

This lie has caused me to feel defeated and stopped me from overcoming sin in my life.

I embrace the truth that God's divine power has given me everything I need for godliness and that I can do all things through Him who gives me strength. In Christ who loves me, I am more than victorious.

Then read the declaration out loud every day for 40 days, all the time reminding yourself that, if God has said it, it really is true. The more you do it, the better.

This is not as easy as it may sound because the lie behind the stronghold *feels* true to you.

Persevere until you have completed at least 40 days—or maybe even more—and remember that throughout most of that time it will feel like a complete waste of time, because the lie feels true to you. If you persevere, you will tear the stronghold down. And you will be transformed.

But this is not about your own efforts. It is about resting in His grace and taking Him at His word. If you miss a day or two, God is not cross with you! Just pick up where you left off and keep going.

Just do one stronghold-buster at a time. Tearing down strongholds is an endurance race, not a sprint. Once one has been demolished, then you can begin busting the next stronghold.

In conclusion, we want to leave you with 1 Peter 1:13: "Prepare your minds for action" (NASB). By renewing your mind, bringing it into alignment with God's truth—what He says about Himself and what He says about you—you will be much better equipped to serve God in this world and bear abundant fruit for His kingdom.

But again, it's not by our own efforts. The verse continues, ". . . set your hope on the grace to be brought to you when Jesus Christ is revealed" (NIV). The grace God showed us when Jesus went to the cross, and the grace He will show us when Jesus returns, is the same grace He shows us day by day to help us renew our minds and walk with Him in this world.

REFLECT

Begin to create your very own stronghold-buster so that you can go on to demolish it. Use the guidelines in this Participant's Guide and take note of the sample stronghold-busters. You can also use the Stronghold-Buster Builder in our apps.

STRONGHOLD-BUSTING SUMMARY

The weapons we fight with are not the weapons of the world. On the contrary, they have divine power to demolish strongholds. We demolish arguments and every pretension that sets itself up against the knowledge of God, and we take captive every thought to make it obedient to Christ. (2 Corinthians 10:4–5 NIV)

Ingrained habitual ways of thinking become deep ruts in our minds. The Bible calls them "strongholds." God's clear promise is that we can demolish them and be set free to think according to the truth. During *The Steps To Experiencing Grace,* you resolved the spiritual issues that the Holy Spirit revealed to you, and this will make it much easier to change ingrained ways of thinking than it was before.

Ongoing transformation will come only as you choose daily to renew your mind (Romans 12:2), that is to say, as you replace ingrained faulty beliefs with what God tells you in the Bible is actually true.

We strongly recommend that you ask God to show you one key belief that you now realize is false and use the following "Stronghold-Busting" process to demolish it over the coming weeks. Once you have replaced that lie with truth, do the same with another false belief, and then another as the Holy Spirit leads you.

1. Identify the Faulty Belief You Want to Change

This is what the Bible calls taking captive every thought to make it obedient to Christ. It means noticing what we are thinking and saying, and considering whether it is in line with what God tells us is true in His Word.

2. Consider What Effect Believing That Lie Is Having in Your Life

Realizing the negative effects should spur us on to tear the stronghold down as we understand the positive changes that will bring.

3. Make a List of Key Bible Verses That Counteract the Lie

Your past experiences may, for example, have left you with a sense that you are helpless and that it would be hopeless to try to change. But God's Word makes some clear statements that contradict that: God will never leave you or forsake you (Isaiah 41:10–13, Hebrews 13:5–6); You can do all things through Jesus who gives you strength (Philippians 4:13).

4. Write a Declaration Based on the Verses

Use the following pattern:

I refuse to believe the lie that . . . [e.g., I am dirty]

Believing this lie has . . . [e.g., given me a deep sense of shame, made me avoid people, etc.]

I embrace the truth that . . . [e.g., I have been washed clean by the blood of Jesus, I am pure and holy, I can draw near to God in full assurance, etc.]

5. Read the Declaration Out Loud Every Day for 40 Days

The Bible says that "the tongue has the power of life and death" (Proverbs 18:21 NIV)! Speaking out loud seems to help our minds take hold of the truth more effectively than simply reading silently.

Be warned! Stronghold-Busting is not as easy as it may sound because the lie behind the stronghold feels absolutely true to you. So, by definition, it will feel for some time as if you are wasting your time.

However, as you go through your 40 days, it's like a concrete wall being demolished. It withstands 10, 20, 30 blows of a sledgehammer with no visible sign of being weakened. As you work through it day after day, it will feel as if nothing is changing. However, eventually a few small cracks appear, and then the cracks get bigger, and finally the wall completely collapses. Even though only the final few blows appear to have had an effect, without the previous blows, the wall would not have fallen. Persevere until the stronghold has been demolished and you really do know the truth that will set you free!

STRONGHOLD-BUSTER EXAMPLE 1

FEAR OF DISAPPROVAL

The lie: I am unacceptable or just not good enough.

Effects in my life: feeling intimidated, fearing people, compromising my convictions, changing my appearance, anxious about saying and doing the "right thing"

The truth:

You did not choose me, but I chose you. (John 15:16)

[He] has also put his seal on us and given us his Spirit in our hearts as a guarantee. (2 Corinthians 1:22)

He will rejoice over you with gladness; he will quiet you by his love; he will exult over you with loud singing. (Zephaniah 3:17)

Man looks on the outward appearance, but the LORD looks on the heart. (1 Samuel 16:7)

The LORD is on my side; I will not fear. What can man do to me? (Psalm 118:6)

We have been approved by God to be entrusted with the gospel, so we speak, not to please man, but to please God who tests our hearts. (1 Thessalonians 2:4)

Dear Father God,

I refuse to believe the lie that I am unacceptable or not good enough.

Believing this lie has caused me to feel intimidated, to fear people, to compromise my convictions, to change my appearance, and to be overanxious about saying and doing the "right thing."

I embrace the truth that You chose me and that I have received a new heart and therefore I have Your seal of approval. Even when others are not pleased with me, You take great delight in me and Your opinion matters much more.

I now choose to please You rather than other people and rely on Your promise to be with me wherever I go as I share the good news with others.

Amen.

1	2	3	4	5	6	7	8	9
10	11	12	13	14	15	16	17	18
19	20	21	22	23	24	25	26	27
28	29	30	31	32	33	34	35	36
37	38	39	40					

STRONGHOLD-BUSTER EXAMPLE 2

FEAR OF FAILURE

The lie: When I fail I am worth less than before.

Effects in my life: being unwilling to attempt new challenges that are outside my comfort zone, being task-focused rather than people-focused, anger, competitiveness, striving for perfection

The truth:

You are precious in my eyes and I love you. (Isaiah 43:4)

In [Christ] you have been made complete. (Colossians 2:10 NASB)

We are his workmanship, created in Christ Jesus for good works, which God prepared beforehand. (Ephesians 2:10)

[God] is able to do far more abundantly than all that we ask or think, according to the power at work within us. (Ephesians 3:20)

It is God who works in you, both to will and to work for his good pleasure. (Philippians 2:13)

Dear Heavenly Father,

I refuse to believe the lie that when I fail I am worth less than before.

Believing this lie has caused me not to attempt new things, to focus on tasks rather than people, to strive for perfection, and to feel angry and competitive.

I embrace the truth that I have been handcrafted by You and am precious, honored, and loved by You regardless of the success or failure of what I do. I declare that I am already fully complete in Christ and that You are working in me for Your good pleasure and to do far more abundantly than all I could ask or think.

In Jesus' name. Amen.

1	2	3	4	5	6	7	8	9
10	11	12	13	14	15	16	17	18
19	20	21	22	23	24	25	26	27
28	29	30	31	32	33	34	35	36
37	38	39	40					

STRONGHOLD-BUSTER EXAMPLE 3

FEELING IRRESISTIBLY DRAWN TO PORN

The lie: I cannot resist the temptation to look at porn.

Effects in my life: deep sense of shame, warped sexual feelings, unable to relate to other people as God intended, harm to my marriage

The truth:

In the same way, count yourselves dead to sin but alive to God in Christ Jesus. Therefore do not let sin reign in your mortal body so that you obey its evil desires. Do not offer any part of yourself to sin as an instrument of wickedness, but rather offer yourselves to God as those who have been brought from death to life; and offer every part of yourself to him as an instrument of righteousness. For sin shall no longer be your master, because you are not under the law, but under grace. (Romans 6:11–14 NIV)

Do you not know that your body is a temple of the Holy Spirit? (1 Corinthians 6:19)

No temptation has overtaken you except what is common to mankind. And God is faithful; he will not let you be tempted beyond what you can bear. But when you are tempted, he will also provide a way out so that you can endure it. (1 Corinthians 10:13 NIV)

So I say, walk by the Spirit, and you will not gratify the desires of the flesh. (Galatians 5:16 NIV)

But the fruit of the Spirit is love, joy, peace, patience, kindness, goodness, faithfulness, gentleness, self-control. (Galatians 5:22–23)

I refuse to believe the lie that I cannot resist the temptation to look at porn.

Believing this lie has given me a deep sense of shame, warped my sexual desires, prevented me from relating to other people as God intended, and harmed my relationship with my spouse.

I embrace the truth that God will always provide a way out when I am tempted, and I will choose to take it. I announce the truth that if I live by the Spirit—and I choose to do that—I will not gratify the desires of the flesh and the fruit of the Spirit, including self-control, will grow in me. I count myself dead to sin and refuse to let sin reign in my body or be my master. Today and every day I give my body to God as a temple of the Holy Spirit to be used only for what honors Him.

I declare that the power of sin is broken in me. I choose to submit completely to God and resist the devil, who must flee from me now.

1	2	3	4	5	6	7	8	9
10	11	12	13	14	15	16	17	18
19	20	21	22	23	24	25	26	27
28	29	30	31	32	33	34	35	36
37	38	39	40					

MAKE FRUITFUL DISCIPLES

CAN WE HELP YOUR CHURCH?

Most Christian leaders want to build communities that are healthy, growing, and full of life. So, it can be frustrating and discouraging when—despite trying everything—the reality falls short of the dream. We understand the discipleship journey can feel like hard work.

All too often, the problem is a culture of immaturity. If Christians in a community lack the desire or direction to take ownership of their spiritual growth, then it's hard to achieve any meaningful momentum.

Freedom In Christ's discipleship resources give church leaders and their churches a proven road map to spiritual maturity that makes discipleship a joy, not a burden, and empowers people to disciple others.

As a result, leaders gain renewed energy in their calling as they grow flourishing communities of lifelong disciples, fulfill God's purposes, and make a difference in the world.

OUR DISCIPLESHIP APPROACH

We eschew "try harder" or "behave better" messages and replace them with simple, powerful, biblical principles for life that anyone, anywhere, anytime can use and pass on to others.

TRUTH: Come to know the incredible love of God in your heart not just your head; know just who you now are in Christ; understand the nature of the spiritual battle and the resources you have in Christ to stand firm.

TURNING: Understand and practice repentance so that you ruthlessly close any doors you've opened to the enemy through past sin and don't open any more.

TRANSFORMATION: Learn practically how to renew your mind by replacing faulty beliefs that have developed with the truth from God's Word.

A LONG-TERM WHOLE-CHURCH STRATEGY

Our discipleship resources provide a proven road map to spiritual maturity that releases disciples to make disciples.

We have testimonies from thousands of Christian leaders who have achieved transformational results with Freedom In Christ.

We do not offer a "one size fits all" approach but love to help each church team identify their specific calling and gifting and select the tools that are appropriate for their own situation.

We provide a self-guided process that's clearly explained and, in many countries, a network of local people who can "train your trainers" and support you every step of the way.

Our discipleship approach is infinitely transferable. Anyone can learn these principles and use them to grow and disciple others. This means that you can quickly and easily build a team to transform discipleship in your church.

We have a particular heart—and highly effective programs—to equip leaders personally.

THE DISCIPLESHIP HUB—ALL OUR RESOURCES TOGETHER IN ONE PLACE

Designed specifically for church and small group leaders, this online platform houses all of Freedom In Christ's material and offers a seamless and user-friendly experience.

It includes not just the videos but access to the accompanying notes, all in an easy-to-use format.

Use it to run small groups—there are tools for interaction, monitoring activity, and communication—or to give individuals access to the courses.

TAKING IT FORWARD

New to Freedom In Christ? Try it for yourself by taking the Freedom In Christ Course or joining our 10-month *Transform* program for leaders.

Looking for more? Choose from our library of courses for you, your team, or your church.

Join our Leaders Community on social media.

More information at: FreedomInChrist.org/Leaders

FREEDOM IN CHRIST'S DISCIPLESHIP COURSES FOR ALL

THE FREEDOM IN CHRIST COURSE

"Men, women, and middle and high school students have been radically transformed."

Bob Huisman, Pastor, Immanuel Christian Reformed Church, Hudsonville, MI, USA

"I recommend it highly to anyone serious about discipleship."

Chuah Seong Peng, Senior Pastor, Holy Light Presbyterian Church, Johor Baru, Malaysia

"The Freedom In Christ Course changed me and put me in a position to minister to people in a much more effective way."

Frikkie Elstadt, Every Nation Patria, Mossel Bay, South Africa

"Our church has changed as a result of this course. Those who come to Christ and who do the course end up with a rock-solid start to their faith."

Pastor Sam Scott, Eltham Baptist Church, Australia

Now in its third edition and translated into well over 40 languages, *The Freedom In Christ Course* can transform the way you help Christians become fruitful disciples. It is our main discipleship resource, and versions are available for different ages so that you can run the same teaching across all ages at the same time.

Focused on first establishing every Christian in the sure foundation of their identity in Jesus, it gives them the tools to break free and stay free from all that holds them back, and a strategy for ongoing transformation.

It has ten teaching sessions presented by Steve Goss, Nancy Maldonado, and Daryl Fitzgerald plus *The Steps To Freedom In Christ* ministry component presented by Steve Goss and Neil Anderson.

Unique to Freedom In Christ, *The Steps To Freedom In Christ* is a powerful step-by-step prayer repentance process that enables participants to resolve their personal and spiritual conflicts by submitting to God and resisting the devil, thereby experiencing their freedom in Christ (James 4:7). It is a gentle and straightforward process just between the participant and God, during which participants uncover "strongholds" that they have developed in their thinking that can be addressed through renewing their mind.

With a specially designed app, extra teaching films, a worship album, a Leader's Guide, a Participant's Guide, and tons of extras, The Freedom In Christ Course offers you everything you need to make disciples who bear fruit that will last!

KEYS TO HEALTH, WHOLENESS, & FRUITFULNESS

"It has given me such freedom to realize that my identity is not tied to any disease, and I don't have to 'own' it."

"I've had some issues about feeling worthless because of what people have said in my past. I looked at the Scriptures and found out who I really am in Christ. That's just really transformed me!"

"This course has made me realize how God heals not only spiritually but through my doctor as well."

"We're surrounded by 'good advice' about health, and you never really know what to believe. A true understanding of wholeness came through from both the medical and the spiritual sense."

Keys To Health, Wholeness, & Fruitfulness is a video-based discipleship course for every Christian. Written and presented by Steve Goss, Dr. Mary Wren, and Dr. Ifeoma Monye, it brings together truth from the Bible and wisdom from the medical world to equip you to be a healthy, whole disciple of Jesus whose life really counts.

The objective of the course is to understand that good physical health is not an end in itself, but a means to help us be and do all that God intends for us as fruitful disciples of Jesus. A complete answer comes only by considering the whole person—spirit, mind, and body.

Dr. Mary Wren, co-author of this course, is a practicing medical doctor. As a student, she had serious illnesses during which she started to learn how to seek God for help and wisdom as well as seeking medical help. She sees herself as a bridge between medicine and the Church.

- Understand how to look after your whole being—spirit, mind, and body.
- Uncover the roots of health issues and learn to resolve them.
- Live well despite the limitations of your physical body.
- Get rid of stress, anxiety, and fear.
- Learn how to make consistent, healthy choices.
- Deal with negative habits that try to control you.
- Understand what the Bible teaches about healing.
- Discover why physical death holds no fear.

The course includes an 8-point plan to ensure you've done everything you're responsible to do for healing, and the *Steps To Healing & Wholeness*.

DEDICATED COURSES FOR YOUNGER GENERATIONS

We understand discipling the next generation requires a different approach. At Freedom In Christ we have developed custom courses that address different age cohorts with a number of courses dedicated to their specific age group and needs.

Our courses range from a course for those in their 20s and 30s, a new course for 11- to 18-year-olds, and a course written specifically by children's ministers for 5- to 11-year-olds.

THE LIGHTBRINGERS

ACTION-PACKED RESOURCE WITH TEN TEACHING SESSIONS FOR CHILDREN AGES 5 TO 11 IN TWO AGE GROUPS (5–7 AND 8–11).

The Lightbringers is a fantastic resource to help children understand their identity in Christ and show them how to view the rest of the world through that lens. It helps children come to know who they are in Jesus and equips them as they grow into young adults.

In this interactive and immersive course, videos with action-packed stories bring biblical truth to life through "The Adventures of Lily Pepper" for kids 5–7 and "The Lightbringers" for kids 8–11. There are also specially written praise and worship songs for each session.

The course incorporates all three "Ts" of the Freedom In Christ approach, including an interactive children's version of *The Steps To Freedom In Christ* called *The Lightbringers Trail*.

Written by Mark Griffiths and Joanne Foster, both specialists in children's ministry, it is designed to equip children to become fruitful disciples and stay connected with Jesus into their adult lives.

The Church Edition contains everything a church needs: a comprehensive hard copy Leader's Guide and online access to downloadable videos, songs, activity sheets, and PowerPoint presentations. Use it with as many children as you like for as long as you like without paying any more.

The Family Edition is a slimmed-down version designed for use on a tablet by parents at home.

iGEN

FREEDOM IN CHRIST FOR YOUNG PEOPLE AGES 11 TO 18.

Reaching today's youth with the gospel of Jesus Christ and the message of Freedom In Christ is vital, and spreading the gospel is not just an older generation to younger generation plan.

iGEN is a discipleship resource designed to set young believers free to reach their generation with the good news of Jesus and the message of identity-based discipleship.

It is designed to draw out participant conversation in spaces that are safe, unpressured, and nonjudgmental. Participants will have opportunities to ask questions, express faith or doubts, and share their personal struggles and victories. Live interaction combined with clearly communicated truth will produce positive spiritual impact.

Hosted exclusively on our Discipleship Hub platform, iGen consists of:

- Ten sessions based on *The Freedom In Christ Course*
- A youth version of *The Steps to Freedom In Christ*.
- Accessed online via devices.
- Video presented by an international cast of excellent communicators.
- Each iGen session has embedded breaks for group interaction and discussions.

iGEN works in a variety of youth contexts. The Leader's Guide will help you to adapt it to your specific needs.

A version in Spanish is also available.

DISCIPLE
FOR 20S AND 30S

"You really get us and understand us; you don't just patronize us and talk down to us."

"God is doing incredible things in the young people at our church and I'm just grateful this course has been able to facilitate that."

"Thank you so much for caring enough to do this. You have no idea how much it means to us that you have taken the time to understand and help us overcome all the stuff that comes at us."

"Disciple is so user-friendly. The young adults really engaged, and there were definite light-bulb moments. The Freedom In Christ message comes across, but in a different way than the Freedom In Christ Course. It's been three months since we did it, and everyone still refers to it."

Church leaders report that discipling those in their 20s and 30s is one of their biggest challenges. *Disciple* is a powerful tool to help you. It speaks the language of the 20s and 30s and invites them to dive into the greatest story ever told, God's story. They will learn how to take hold of their freedom and discover their mandate from God.

- Ten sessions designed to run for approximately 90 minutes each
- Impactful Starter Films introduce the theme for each session
- Extra films (via the app) on topics including Sex, the Occult, and Fear
- Chat and Reflect times allow teaching to take root
- App with extra teaching films, daily devotional, daily nuggets of extra teaching, and Stronghold–Buster Builder with reminders

COURSES DESIGNED BY CHRISTIAN LEADERS FOR CHRISTIAN LEADERS

TRANSFORM

A PERSONAL JOURNEY FOR CHRISTIAN LEADERS INTO GREATER FREEDOM, FRUITFULNESS, AND DISCIPLE-MAKING.

"TRANSFORM succeeded in mending gaps in my spiritual life, and repositioned me for the various tasks ahead of me. I would highly recommend it to any leader."

"I would strongly recommend it to any Christian in a leadership position, whether it's in church, ministry, public service, or business. It's a wonderful opportunity for personal growth in intimacy with God, in a safe setting, with excellent input and fellowship—something I've rarely found as a leader."

"God uses different tools to sharpen us. TRANSFORM is one of those tools. It's a journey where you dive into truths and are deeply challenged to be more like Jesus."

TRANSFORM is specifically designed for church leaders and leaders of Christian organizations who are passionate about leading a church or ministry of fruitful disciples that makes a major impact for the Kingdom of God.

It will help you ground your leadership firmly in the biblical principles of identity, freedom, and transformation and equip you to go even deeper into God personally, confident that this will lead to greater influence and fruitfulness in your life and ministry. You will then be well placed to kick-start or accelerate the process of personal and corporate discipleship in your church.

TRANSFORM is a 9-month program of weekly study, reflection, and fellowship run online by Freedom In Christ using Zoom conferencing and two retreats. Guided and directed by a dedicated Transform leader, you will go through three stages—*Reposition*, *Retune*, and *Refocus*—with a "community" of like-minded leaders all traveling through the Transform journey. There will be an abundance of sharing, discussion, and prayer throughout the process.

FREED TO LEAD

"It has reinforced my conviction that my identity is first and foremost in Christ, whatever leadership role I may hold."

"The Freed To Lead *course has been the most amazing leadership development experience of my career, having been called to both marketplace and church leadership for over 20 years. It dispels worldly leadership myths and practices and provides biblical foundations for godly leadership. I wholeheartedly recommend this course for anyone who aspires or is currently called to godly servant-hearted leadership in any arena."*

"An outstanding course—inspirational and motivational, affirming and encouraging."

At a time of complex leadership challenges in churches, where Christian leaders face huge obstacles and struggle to balance corporate and Christian leadership styles, *Freed To Lead* will help you lead out of your identity in Christ.

It's a powerful 10-week video-led discipleship course for Christians who are called to leadership—whether in the marketplace, public service, the Church, or any other context. *Freed to Lead* shows how being rooted in Christ is the true foundation for all Christians with responsibility for leading or managing others.

Written by Christian leaders for Christian leaders, it will transform your approach to leadership, free you from drivenness and burnout, enable you to survive personal attacks, use conflict positively, and overcome other barriers to effective leadership.

Freed to Lead will help you discover how to develop a healthy approach to leadership and stay on course to achieve your God-given vision.

Church leadership teams will benefit hugely from going through it together before rolling it out to others in their church who are in leadership in any sphere or think they may be called to leadership in the future.

- 10–session course or retreat plus *The Steps To Freedom For Leaders*
- A dedicated *Freed to Lead* book by Christian author and church leader Rod Woods
- An excellent follow–up to *The Freedom In Christ Course* and *The Grace Course*
- Video testimonies and "Pause For Thought" discussion times

BECOME A FRIEND OF FREEDOM IN CHRIST

Freedom In Christ Ministries was founded over 30 years ago by Dr. Neil T. Anderson. We offer a unique approach to discipleship based on our three core principles of Truth, Turning, and Transformation.

Now based in 40 countries with translations in over 30 languages, Freedom In Christ has equipped millions of Christians worldwide to cultivate a lifestyle of unstoppable spiritual growth.

WILL YOU STAND WITH US?

Have you seen people's lives transformed through this course? Would you like to be involved in making the impact even greater? If you are excited about the effect this teaching can have on individuals, churches, and communities, we'd love to have you on the team!

JOIN OUR TEAM OF INTERNATIONAL SUPPORTERS

Freedom In Christ exists to equip the Church worldwide to make fruitful disciples. We rely heavily for financial support on people who have understood how important it is to give leaders the tools that will enable them to help people become fruitful disciples, not just converts, especially when we are opening up an office in a new country.

Typically your support will be used to:

- help us equip church leaders around the world
- open Freedom In Christ offices in new countries
- translate our discipleship resources into other languages
- develop new discipleship resources

JOIN THE TEAM OF SUPPORTERS IN YOUR COUNTRY

We are passionate about working with those who have themselves been touched by the biblical message of freedom. Financial support enables us to develop new resources and get them into the hands of more church leaders. As a result many, many people are connecting with this life-changing message. There are always new projects—small and large—that don't happen unless there's funding for them.

To find out more about partnering with us please go to:

FreedomInChrist.org/Friends

LIES LIST

Use this space to make a list of areas where you realize that your belief system has not been in line with what God says is true in His Word. Record the lie in the left-hand column and, if you can, use the right-hand column to record what is actually true from the Bible. You will have opportunity to address them using Stronghold-Busting.

Remember, you are transformed by the renewal of your mind (Romans 12:2). Identifying faulty thinking and replacing it with what is actually true is a crucial part of *The Grace Course*. It takes effort, but it's well worth it!

LIE	TRUTH
Example: I am dirty	I have been washed clean by the blood of the Lamb (Revelation 7:14)